The Ultimate

Washington
REDSKINS
TRIVIA
BOOK

By David Elfin

21st Century Online Publishing

Cover photo of Gus Frerotte courtesy of Washington Redskins/Bill Wood. Cover photos of Sonny Jurgensen and Sammy Baugh courtesy of Washington Redskins

Dedication

To my daughters, Julie and Amy, who are my soul and inspiration.

Acknowledgements

I would like to acknowledge several people without whom this book could not have been written. First and foremost is my friend and business manager, Rick Snider. I would also like to thank my boss, Gary Hopkins, and my Washington Times colleagues Dan Daly and Dick Heller. Mike McCall of the Redskins contributed greatly to this project as did Pete Fierle of the Pro Football Hall of Fame. I can't measure my gratitude to my wife, Loretta Garcia, and my parents, Mel and Margery Elfin. And special thanks to David Jones, John Johnston and all the folks at American Sports Media and Whitehall Printing.

David Elfin
Bethesda, Md.
March 31, 1998

To order additional copies, call 1-800-408-8379

TABLE OF CONTENTS

RB JOHN RIGGINS (1976-79, 81-85)   *Photo courtesy of the Washington Redskins*

SIX DECADES OF SUCCESS

ALL-TIME REDSKINS TEAM

OFFENSE

MARK MOSELEY
(K)

BRIAN MITCHELL
(KR)

LARRY BROWN
(RB)

JOHN RIGGINS
(RB)

SONNY JURGENSEN
(QB)

CHARLEY TAYLOR	JOE JACOBY	RUSS GRIMM	LEN HAUSS	VINCE PROMUTO	TURK EDWARDS	JERRY SMITH	ART MONK
(WR)	(T)	(G)	(C)	(G)	(T)	(TE)	(WR)

DEFENSE

DE	DT	DT	DE
DEXTER MANLEY	DAVE BUTZ	DIRON TALBERT	GENE BRITO

CB
DARRELL GREEN

CB
PAT FISCHER

LB	LB	LB
CHRIS HANBURGER	CHUCK DRAZENOVICH	KEN HARVEY

S	S
KEN HOUSTON	PAUL KRAUSE

P
SAMMY BAUGH

COACH
JOE GIBBS

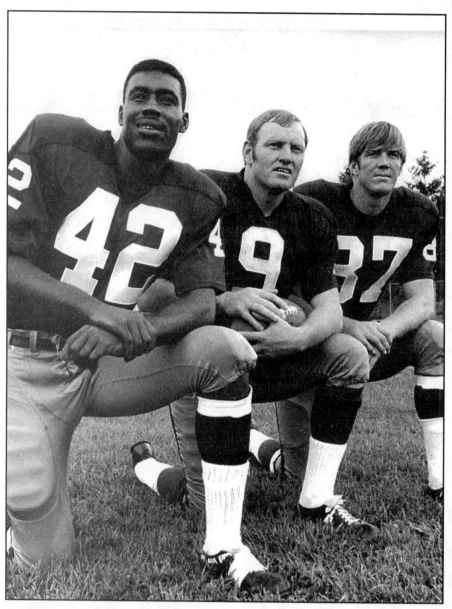

(L-R) WR CHARLEY TAYLOR (1964-77), QB SONNY JURGENSEN (1964-74), AND TE JERRY SMITH (1965-77) *Photo courtesy of the Washington Redskins*

Washington's Best
OFFENSE

Sonny Jurgensen (1964-74) —*One of the game's purest passers.*

John Riggins (1976-79, 81-85) —*No runner was better after 30.*

Larry Brown (1969-76) —*Maybe the NFL's most unappreciated back.*

Art Monk (1980-93) —*Mr. Consistency was the model Redskin.*

Charley Taylor (1964-77) —*Graceful receiver and brutal blocker.*

Jerry Smith (1965-77) —*Prototype receiving tight end.*

Joe Jacoby (1981-93) —*Was league's top left tackle from 1983-86.*

Turk Edwards (1937-40) —*Hall of Famer later coached Redskins.*

Russ Grimm (1981-91) —*Was heart of famed Hogs line.*

Vince Promuto (1960-70) —*Down era couldn't hide his greatness.*

Len Hauss (1964-77) —*6 straight Pro Bowls, 192 straight starts.*

Mark Moseley (1974-86) —*Only kicker to be named the NFL's MVP.*

Brian Mitchell (1990-) —*Led league in total yards from 1994-96.*

DEFENSE

Dexter Manley (1981-89) —*Rewrote club record book for sacks.*

Gene Brito (1951-53, 55-58) —*5 Pro Bowls for '50s bright spot.*

Dave Butz (1975-88) —*Big man missed 2 games in last 11 years.*

Diron Talbert (1971-80) —*Leader of '70s Over the Hill gang.*

Ken Harvey (1994-97) —*4 years, 4 Pro Bowls.*

Chris Hanburger (1965-78) —*Redskins record 9 Pro Bowls.*

Chuck Drazenovich (1950-59) —*4 straight Pro Bowls.*

Darrell Green (1983-) —*Ageless one was still on top at 37.*

Pat Fischer (1968-77) —*Fierce desire overcame small stature.*

Ken Houston (1973-80) —*Made Redskins' most memorable tackle.*

Paul Krause (1964-67) —*The model ballhawking free safety.*

Sammy Baugh (1937-52) —*Defined the Redskins for 16 years.*

Joe Gibbs (1981-92) —*3 Super Bowl titles, 10 winning seasons.*

QB SONNY JURGENSEN (1964-74)   *Photo courtesy of the Washington Redskins*

SONNY JURGENSEN

He wasn't a great athlete, not with that everyday man's physique. His teams weren't champions, not with just three winning records in his 11 seasons as a first-stringer.

But few quarterbacks in NFL history have ever thrown the ball the way Sonny Jurgensen did. Almost a quarter-century after his retirement from the Redskins in 1974, Jurgensen still ranked in the top 10 alltime in both quarterback rating and touchdown passes. The only passers ahead of him in both categories were Dan Marino and Joe Montana.

While playing at Duke, Jurgensen once completed a pass behind his back for 37 yards. Redskins Hall of Fame receiver Charley Taylor claimed Jurgensen could throw a slider, making the football curl around a defender.

And yet, less than two years after he had led the NFL in passing yards for a second straight season, Philadelphia traded Jurgensen to Washington. The Eagles had beaten the Redskins in four of the six meetings during Jurgensen's three years as their starter. They would win just three of 22 during Jurgensen's 11 seasons in Washington.

"It was the best thing that ever happened to me," Jurgensen said of the 1964 trade which had initially been such a shock.

The Redskins usually didn't have much of a running game or a defense during Jurgensen's era. However, the team's lack of success didn't prevent the redhead from becoming a Washington icon for his passing wizardry and his fearlessness in the face of huge deficits.

In 1965, the Redskins trailed the Dallas Cowboys 21-0, but won 34-31 as Jurgensen threw two touchdown passes in the final four minutes. Jurgensen and Washington set an NFL regular-season record by scoring 72 points against the New York Giants in 1966. And in his final season, the 40-year-old Jurgensen brought the Redskins from behind in the fourth quarter to beat two-time Super Bowl champion Miami.

From 1948-71, 24 quarterbacks passed for 400 yards in a game once. Two passers managed it twice. Jurgensen did so five times.

Johnny Unitas was a peerless leader. No quarterback won more often than Otto Graham. But as Cowboys Hall of Fame cornerback Mel Renfro said, "When it comes down to pure passers, there's no question Sonny was the best."

PASSING FANCY

1. Who holds the Redskins' record for most passing yards in a season?

2. Sonny Jurgensen set the club record with 32 completions in a game against Cleveland in 1967. Who tied the mark?

3. Who holds the Redskins' career record for completions?

4. Who holds the club record for yards passing in a game?

5. Sammy Baugh threw six touchdown passes against Brooklyn in 1943 and the Chicago Cardinals in 1947. Who equalled that feat?

6. Which Redskin threw the most interceptions in a season?

7. Who holds the Redskins' record for career completion percentage?

8. Who passed for the most yards in a game against Washington?

9. Which two passers tied the NFL record by throwing seven touchdown passes in games against the Redskins?

10. Who attempted the most passes in a game against the Redskins?

Bonus: Who's the only Redskins' quarterback besides Hall of Famers Baugh and Jurgensen to lead the NFL in passing?

THE NICKNAMES

1. Which Redskins defensive lineman was dubbed "The Dancing Bear"?

2. This Redskins halfback was called "Choo Choo." Name him.

3. This Redskins runner was as powerful as a locomotive.

4. What Redskins quarterback was called "Whiskey"?

5. No one called this Hall of Fame lineman by his given name of Albert. Who was he?

6. A star at Virginia, this running back wasn't as fast as his nickname implied. Name him.

7. Which kick returner earned his rapid-sounding sobriquet?

8. He only carried the ball for Washington in 1987, but "L-Train" had a big impact. Who was he?

9. This Redskins offensive lineman was nicknamed "Stinky." Name him.

10. What great Redskins receiver was dubbed "Bones?'

Bonus: What's Sonny Jurgensen's given name?

THE HALL OF FAMERS

1. Name the Hall of Fame defensive lineman who finished his career with the Redskins in 1974.

2. How many Hall of Fame coaches worked for the Redskins?

3. Who were Washington's first two Hall of Famers?

4. How many Hall of Famers have Redskins connections?

5. How many Hall of Famers were part of the 1937 Redskins?

6. Name the three Hall of Famers whom the Redskins coaxed out of retirement.

7. From what team did the Redskins hire Hall of Fame coach Joe Gibbs?

8. Name the Hall of Fame quarterback who didn't fare well as Washington's coach.

9. What Hall of Fame defensive tackle closed out his 13-year career with a season in Washington (1966)?

10. Which Hall of Famer played the most games for Washington?

Bonus: Only three Hall of Famers spent their entire NFL careers with the Washington (not Boston) Redskins. Name them.

WELCOME TO WASHINGTON

1. Where did the Redskins play before moving to Washington?

2. Who were the team's rookie stars in its first season?

3. What was the club's original home stadium?

4. Why did the club move to Washington?

5. Who scored all the Redskins' points in their D.C. debut?

6. For whom was Griffith Stadium named?

7. What was the name of Washington's previous NFL team?

8. How many consecutive winning home seasons did the Redskins have after arriving in Washington in 1937?

9. How many home playoff games did the Redskins play during their 24 seasons in Griffith Stadium?

10. Which team did the Redskins beat for their final victory at Griffith?

Bonus: What was the seating capacity for football at Griffith?

QB SAMMY BAUGH (1937-52)   *Photo courtesy of the Washington Redskins*

SAMMY BAUGH

The Redskins had played for the NFL championship in 1936, but few people in Boston cared. Owner George Preston Marshall decided to move the club to Washington in hopes of attracting bigger crowds. But Marshall also knew he needed a colorful star.

Marshall found him in the first round of the 1937 draft. However, lanky Texas Christian quarterback Sammy Baugh signed with baseball's St. Louis Cardinals rather than accept Marshall's contract. With the NFL season approaching, Marshall finally relented and offered $8,000, easily the highest salary on the Redskins.

Baugh, who gave up baseball in 1939 because he couldn't hit curveballs, proved to be worth every dollar. After his first practice, Washington Hall of Fame coach Ray Flaherty finished diagramming a play by telling Baugh to hit the receiver in the eye with the ball. Baugh asked, "Which eye?"

Baugh, who led the Redskins to their first championship in 1937 and guided them back to the title game four times in the next eight years, was that good a passer. But "Slinging Sammy" was also the NFL's best quick-kicker and a deft defensive back.

In 1943, Baugh pulled off an unmatched triple crown, leading the league in passing, punting and interceptions. However, Baugh's most famous moment that season didn't come on the field. He suffered a concussion making a tackle and was knocked out of the title game. A photographer caught Baugh crying on the bench as the defending champion Redskins lost 41-21.

"That was the most miserable day I ever spent in pro football," Baugh said later.

Baugh always had a flair for the dramatic. In 1947 when Redskins fans saluted him with the gift of a burgundy station wagon, Baugh returned the affection by setting an NFL record with six touchdown passes to beat the Chicago Cardinals.

The Redskins finished below .500 in all but one of Baugh's final seven years, but he remained a glorious star. Today, 46 years after his final season, Baugh remains atop the NFL record book in 10 categories including: most seasons leading the league in passing; highest average gain per pass in a game; most seasons leading the league in punting; highest punting average in a career and a season; and most interceptions in a game.

Little wonder Baugh was a member of the Hall of Fame's first class in in 1963.

JUST FOR KICKS

1. Who holds the Redskins' record for most punts in a game?

2. Name the four punters the Redskins used in 1988.

3. Who was Washington's punter in Super Bowls XVII and XVIII?

4. Who holds the Redskins' season record with 29 punts inside the 20-yard line?

5. Who averaged a club-record 59.4 yards per-punt in a game?

6. Who's the only Redskin besides Sammy Baugh to lead the NFL in punting?

7. Who succeeded Baugh as Washington's punter in 1948?

8. Which Redskin led the league in punts?

9. Who was Washington's punter in Super Bowl XXVI?

10. Baugh boomed three of Washington's four longest punts. Who kicked the other?

Bonus: Name the other quarterback besides Baugh to serve as Washington's regular punter.

GRAPPLING WITH THE GIANTS

1. Which Redskin did the Giants "steal" in 1992?

2. What happened to Sonny Jurgensen at Yankee Stadium in 1972?

3. What happened to Larry Brown in that same game?

4. What happened at the end of the 1939 NFL Championship Game between the Redskins and Giants in New York?

5. What happened the next time the teams met?

6. What did Jay Schroeder do on his second play after replacing the injured Joe Theismann against the Giants in 1985?

7. What amazing feat did Hall of Fame running back Cliff Battles accomplish against the Giants in New York in 1937?

8. Which Giants kicker beat the Redskins with a 52-yard last-second field goal in 1989 at RFK?

9. Who scored two touchdowns of more than 60 yards in Washington's record-setting 72-41 rout of New York in 1966?

10. Whom did Washington acquire from New York in 1937 to block for rookie quarterback Sammy Baugh?

Bonus: What two things happened to Joe Gibbs on Jan. 11, 1987 that never happened to him in any other game in his Redskins career?

T TURK EDWARDS (1932-40)   *Photo courtesy of the Washington Redskins*

BEST OF 1937-46

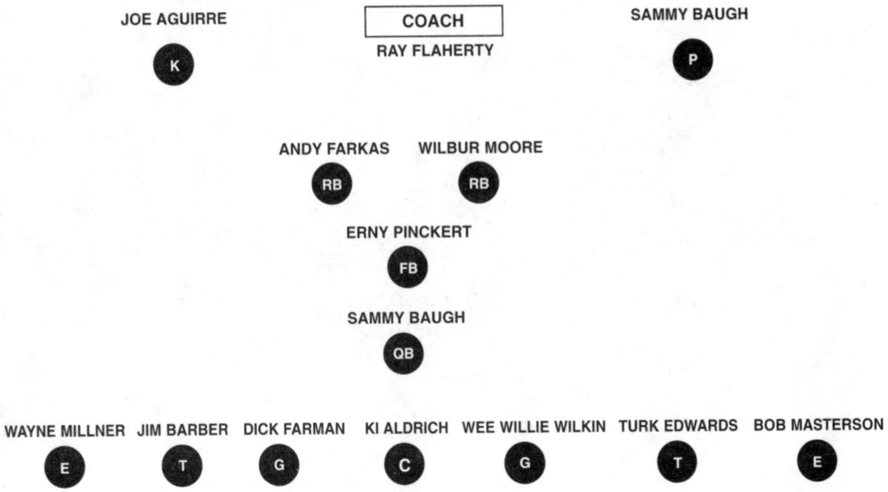

JOE AGUIRRE
K

COACH
RAY FLAHERTY

SAMMY BAUGH
P

ANDY FARKAS
RB

WILBUR MOORE
RB

ERNY PINCKERT
FB

SAMMY BAUGH
QB

WAYNE MILLNER
E

JIM BARBER
T

DICK FARMAN
G

KI ALDRICH
C

WEE WILLIE WILKIN
G

TURK EDWARDS
T

BOB MASTERSON
E

Note: This was football's last fully single platoon era. Players played both offense and defense.

Photo courtesy of the Washington Redskins

OWNER GEORGE PRESTON MARSHALL (1933-63)

GEORGE PRESTON MARSHALL

George Preston Marshall was a showman. Marshall, who always dressed elegantly and traveled by limousine, was a failed actor whose first wife was an ex-chorus girl and whose second wife had been a silent screen siren.

As the Redskins' owner, Marshall proposed a slimmer football and rules changes to encourage passing. Marshall also created the two-division, championship game format and the Pro Bowl. Marshall started the NFL's first marching band and staged halftime shows that were often as entertaining as the games.

Marshall established the Redskins as the entire South's team with an extensive radio network. When television arrived, he made sure the club was the first to have its games shown locally and then regionally.

But none of this may have happened in Washington if Marshall, an heir to a chain of laundries and a sometime Broadway impresario, hadn't been so frustrated by Boston's disinterest in his Eastern Division champion Redskins of 1936. Fed up by poor attendance, Marshall switched the NFL Championship Game to New York and then moved the club to Washington the following spring.

That fall, the Redskins beat the Chicago Bears to win their first title. They would win another in 1942 while finishing second in 1940, 1943 and 1945 and stealing the city's heart away from baseball's Senators. Griffith Stadium was usually sold out on fall Sundays even as the Redskins staggered in the 1950s and Marshall changed coaches on a near bi-annual basis.

So Marshall decided the Redskins needed a bigger stadium. But the price would be high for the bigoted owner, who had made his club the NFL's last to honor the color ban that had permeated pro sports. Since the stadium was being built by the government, which barred discrimination, Marshall was forced to hire black players in 1962. The next year, not long after being elected to the Hall of Fame, the ailing Marshall turned control of the club to three of his board members.

"Mr. Marshall was an outspoken foe of the status quo when most were content with it," NFL commissioner Pete Rozelle said at Marshall's funeral in 1969. "We are all beneficiaries of what his dynamic personality helped shape for more than three decades."

That's especially true in Washington.

THE FRONT OFFICE

1. What was the other main business of George Preston Marshall, the Redskins' first owner?

2. Who wrote "Hail To The Redskins" for Marshall's team?

3. How many coaches did Marshall fire during his last 20 years in charge of the Redskins?

4. What did Marshall's successor, Edward Bennett Williams, say about coach/general manager George Allen's spending habits?

5. Whom did Williams hire to replace Allen in 1978?

6. What other team did Williams buy in 1979, giving up the Redskins to Jack Kent Cooke?

7. Which teams had Cooke previously run?

8. What was remarkable about Cooke's first marriage?

9. Where did Bobby Beathard work after leaving the Redskins?

10. How did general manager Charley Casserly come to the Redskins?

Bonus: Name the sites where Cooke tried to build a new stadium for the Redskins in a near-decade-long search before winding up in Prince George's County in 1996.

GRIFFITH STADIUM (1937-60) *Photo courtesy of the Washington Redskins/Bill Wood*

LB CHUCK DRAZENOVICH (1950-59) *Photo courtesy of the Washington Redskins*

THE SLIDE

BEST OF 1947-56

OFFENSE

DICK POILLON
K

EDDIE SAENZ
KR

VIC JANOWICZ **RB**   CHOO CHOO JUSTICE **RB**

ROB GOODE **FB**

SAMMY BAUGH **QB**

JOHN CARSON	PAUL LIPSCOMB	GENE PEPPER	HARRY ULINSKI	SLUG WITUCKI	LAURIE NIEMI	BONES TAYLOR
E	**T**	**G**	**C**	**G**	**T**	**E**

DEFENSE

DB	DE	DT	DT	DE	DB
DAN SANDIFER	GENE BRITO	VOLNEY PETERS	DICK MODZELEWSKI	JOE TERESHINSKI	HARRY GILMER

LB	LB	LB
CHUCK DRAZENOVICH	AL DEMAO	TORGY TORGESON

DB	DB
SCOOTER SCUDERO	BILL DUDLEY

P	COACH
EDDIE LEBARON	CURLY LAMBEAU

THE REST OF THE LEAGUE

1. Against which team did the Redskins score a club-record 51 points in a playoff game?

2. Which NFC teams have the Redskins never met in the playoffs?

3. Which team hasn't visited Washington since 1979?

4. Which team haven't the Redskins visited since 1985?

5. What non-1995 expansion foe has never beaten Washington?

6. Which team was the last to shut out the Redskins?

7. Which team has Washington faced in a record seven playoff games?

8. Who had the edge during the 15 straight seasons that the Redskins met the Baltimore Colts?

9. Which non-NFC East rival have the Redskins played most often?

10. Which teams have the Redskins never beaten on the road?

Bonus: What did Washington do against Carolina and Jacksonville that no other team did from 1995-97?

PRO BOWL PICKS

1. Which three Redskins were selected for the initial Pro Bowl in 1950?

2. Which Redskin was voted to a club-record nine Pro Bowls?

3. Which Redskin went to five Pro Bowls in the 1950s?

4. What year did the Redskins not have a Pro Bowl player?

5. What player has made the Pro Bowl every year he has been a Redskin?

6. What year did the Redskins have a club-record eight Pro Bowl players?

7. Which Redskin went to the Pro Bowl in each of his first six seasons in Washington?

8. Who's the only Redskin to go to the Pro Bowl at two positions?

9. Who was the last Redskins' rookie to make the Pro Bowl?

10. When did the Redskins' coaches last work the Pro Bowl?

Bonus: Name the four Redskins' special-teamers who have gone to two Pro Bowls.

S PAUL KRAUSE (1964-67)   *Photo courtesy of the Washington Redskins*

PAUL KRAUSE

If Paul Krause had played his entire 16-year career with the Redskins, he would surely hold the club record for interceptions. After all, Krause picked off 81 passes, the most in NFL history.

Unfortunately for Redskins fans, Krause played just four seasons in Washington before being traded to Minnesota in 1968 for linebacker Marlin McKeever and a seventh-round draft choice.

The Redskins were not a good defensive team during Krause's tenure. However, the former all-Big Ten star from Iowa shone from the start. Krause was the runnerup to teammate Charley Taylor for Rookie of the Year honors in 1964 and went to the Pro Bowl in each of his first two seasons. Krause's ballhawking style produced 18 interceptions in 1964-65, but when Otto Graham replaced Bill McPeak as Washington's coach in 1966, he wanted Krause to be more physical and make more tackles. Krause wasn't comfortable with that approach. He slipped to 10 interceptions over the next two years.

"I feel my responsibility is basically to stop the long bomb in the middle of the field," Krause explained. "On running plays, I'm usually the last guy. If he gets by me, it will probably be a touchdown so I just want to get him down rather than going for the big hit."

The Redskins were never winners during Krause's tenure. And the Vikings had finished over .500 once during their first seven seasons. But they captured the NFC Central title in 10 of Krause's 12 seasons in Minnesota, reaching the Super Bowl four times.

Krause's instincts were so sharp that he led the NFC in interceptions at age 33. His hands were so good that Vikings player personnel chief Frank Gilliam said he has never seen a better holder for kicks. Krause's legs were nimble enough that he averaged an astounding 17.7 yards per-interception *after* his 32nd birthday. And he missed just two games in his 16 seasons.

"Paul played the position differently than people in his era," said Vikings Hall of Fame quarterback Fran Tarkenton, a teammate for seven seasons. "He was a true centerfielder. He was a tremendous athlete and he had a great feel for the game."

Which is why Krause went to eight Pro Bowls and was elected to the Hall of Fame in 1998.

PICKING THEM OFF

1. Who holds the Redskins' record for interceptions in a season?

2. Name the two Redskins to pick off four passes in a game.

3. Which Redskin once intercepted a pass in seven straight games?

4. Who holds the club record for interception return yardage?

5. Which linebacker is tied for second in club history with three touchdowns on interception returns?

6. Which quarterback has Redskins career interception leader Darrell Green victimized the most?

7. Which quarterback did the Redskins intercept six times in a game?

8. Which players have picked off four passes in a game against Washington?

9. Which opponent scored two touchdowns on interceptions in a game against the Redskins?

10. Who are the only Redskins since 1964 to lead the NFL in interceptions?

Bonus: Name the four Redskins who have returned two interceptions for touchdowns in a season.

FIGHT FOR OLD D.C.

1. Who built D.C. Stadium?

2. What happened on the first play of the Redskins' opener in their new stadium in 1961?

3. Who scored the first touchdown at D.C. Stadium?

4. Who scored the first Washington touchdown at D.C. Stadium?

5. Who returned an interception for a Redskins touchdown in the stadium's debut?

6. Who scored the game-winning touchdown in the opener?

7. How long did it take the Redskins to win in D.C. Stadium?

8. Who was the hero of that victory?

9. Who was the coach of those 1961 Redskins?

10. How many years did it take before the Redskins finished with a winning record at D.C. Stadium?

Bonus: When was D.C. Stadium renamed RFK Stadium?

WR BOBBY MITCHELL (1962-68)   *Photo courtesy of the Washington Redskins*

THE LONG CLIMB

BEST OF 1957-66

OFFENSE

SAM BAKER
K

DICK JAMES
KR

CHARLEY TAYLOR
RB

DON BOSSELER
RB

SONNY JURGENSEN
QB

BOBBY MITCHELL — WR
FRAN O'BRIEN — T
DICK STANFEL — G
HARRY ULINSKI — C
VINCE PROMUTO — G
ED KHAYAT — T
PAT RICHTER — TE
BILL ANDERSON — WR

DEFENSE

CB	DE	DT	DT	DE	CB
JOHNNY SAMPLE	JOHN PALUCK	BOB TONEFF	JOE RUTGENS	CARL KEMMERER	DALE HACKBART

LB	LB	LB
CHUCK DRAZENOVICH	SAM HUFF	CHRIS HANBURGER

S	S
PAUL KRAUSE	JIM STEFFEN

P
SAM BAKER

COACH
BILL McPEAK

WR ART MONK (1980-93)   *courtesy of the Washington Redskins/Scott Cunningham*

ART MONK

If any player defined the Redskins during their most glorious era, it was Art Monk. He may have set NFL records for catches in a career and in a season, but the humble Monk never crowed about his personal accomplishments.

"A lot of guys have it backwards," Monk said. "They want to do well and hope their team does well. I believed if the team did well, the individual things would take care of themselves."

That unselfish attitude endeared Monk to his teammates and to the Washington fans during his 14 Redskins seasons.

"Art's the greatest . . . a true football player and a true man," said guard Raleigh McKenzie, a teammate for nine years.

Monk was a gifted athlete, but he never stopped working on his game, even after the three Pro Bowls, the three Super Bowl rings and all the records. Monk who "couldn't catch the ball to save my life" when he enrolled at Syracuse as a running back in 1976, left school as a star receiver and Washington's first pick in the first round in 12 years.

With the prodding of veteran halfback Terry Metcalf, who lived across the street during his second season in 1981, Monk became a workout demon. Few teammates ever cared to spend more than a couple of days alongside Monk during his grueling offseason regimen.

"Art wasn't the most muscular or the strongest, but he was always in the best shape," said defensive end Charles Mann, a teammate for 11 seasons. "Art's a self-motivator."

So much so that in 1995, 10 months after having presumably played his last game, the 37-year-old Monk was still working out three hours a day in hopes of catching on with another team. The effort paid off shortly thereafter when he was signed by Philadelphia for whom he made the last six of his 940 catches.

The go-to guy for Redskins quarterbacks from Joe Theismann to Mark Rypien, Monk caught a then-record 104 balls in 1984. He averaged 77 catches his next six full years (not counting strike-shortened 1987) before setting the career mark with his 820th reception in 1992.

"Whenever we needed a clutch play, we looked to Art," Rypien said.

And for 183 straight games over 16 years, if Monk played, he caught a pass. A model of consistency and the model Redskin.

IT'S BETTER TO RECEIVE

1. Who holds the Redskins' record for receiving yards in a game?

2. Who holds the Redskins' record for receiving yards in a season?

3. Four Redskins have caught 12 touchdown passes in a season. Name them.

4. Who holds the Redskins' record for career touchdown catches?

5. Art Monk holds the top three spots on Washington's list for passes caught in a season. Who's fourth?

6. Which two Redskins each recorded 1,000 yards of receiving in a club-record five seasons?

7. Which player caught the most passes in a game against the Redskins?

8. Which player caught four touchdown passes in a game against the Redskins?

9. Who was the last non-wideout to lead the Redskins in receiving before tight end Jamie Asher in 1997?

10. Who holds the record for most receiving yards in a game against the Redskins?

Bonus: Which two Redskins caught a club-record 13 passes in a game?

DUELING WITH DALLAS

1. Who was the Cowboys' first quarterback?

2. Which Dallas coach had a better record against the Redskins: Tom Landry or Jimmy Johnson?

3. Who caught the late touchdown pass in the 1979 finale which gave the Cowboys a 35-34 victory and the NFC East title and knocked the Redskins out of the playoffs?

4. Who scored Washington's touchdowns in its 14-7 victory over Dallas in 1973 that was decided by Ken Houston's goal-line tackle on Walt Garrison?

5. What did many Redskins do before the 1983 game in Dallas?

6. Who scored the replacement Redskins' only touchdown in their stunning 13-7 victory in Dallas in 1987?

7. Which Redskins forced and recovered Troy Aikman's fumble that beat the Cowboys in 1992 at RFK?

8. Who scored the winning points in Washington's come-from-behind 34-31 triumph over Dallas in 1965 in D.C.?

9. Which Redskin was whipped by Drew Pearson for the decisive touchdown pass from Clint Longley in the Cowboys' shocking Thanksgiving Day victory in 1974?

10. What 1972 Redskins starter had begun his career with the Cowboys?

Bonus: What player appeared in both the Redskins-Cowboys NFC Championship Games in 1972 and 1982?

FAREWELL TO RFK

1. Who scored the final touchdown at RFK Stadium?

2. Who scored Washington's final touchdown at RFK?

3. Who teamed up for the last touchdown pass at RFK?

4. Who made the final catch at RFK?

5. Who was the last player to touch the ball at RFK?

6. Who made the final interception at RFK?

7. Who was flagged for the final penalty at RFK?

8. What did Redskins offensive tackle Ed Simmons do to make the RFK finale special?

9. Who was the last opponent to win at RFK?

10. How many opponents finished above .500 at RFK?

Bonus: Which Redskins coach had the best record at RFK?

1. Whose hands first touched a ball in the opening game of Jack Kent Cooke Stadium?

2. Who scored the first points at Cooke Stadium?

3. What was strange about the first touchdown at Cooke Stadium?

4. Who caught the first touchdown pass at Cooke Stadium?

5. Who scored the first rushing touchdown at Cooke Stadium?

6. Who was the first opponent to win at Cooke Stadium?

7. Who made the first interception at Cooke Stadium?

8. Who won the first night game at Cooke Stadium?

9. Who recovered the first fumble at Cooke Stadium?

10. Who scored the first defensive touchdown at Cooke Stadium?

Bonus: Cooke Stadium's construction coincided with the move of the team's training camp to Frostburg State University in Frostburg, Md. Name the Redskins' seven previous summer homes.

CB DARRELL GREEN (1983-)   *Photo courtesy of the Washington Redskins/Bill Wood*

DARRELL GREEN

He may have been a first-round draft choice, but Darrell Green didn't expect to make a huge impact in the NFL. After all, he was a self-described "little-bitty" cornerback from Division II Texas A&I.

Green may have been just 5-foot-8 and 184 pounds, but he got noticed in a hurry. Making his debut as a starter for defending Super Bowl champion Washington on Monday Night Football against archrival Dallas in 1983, Green used all of his world-class speed to become the first player to chase down Cowboys all-Pro halfback Tony Dorsett from behind.

Green, who would win the NFL's fastest man competition three times, never stopped running or working on his coverage skills. He made the Pro Bowl in 1984 and has been back to Hawaii six times. Green's selections at ages 36 and 37 in 1996 and 1997 made him the oldest cornerback ever given such acclaim.

Along the way, Green has helped the Redskins win two Super Bowls and reach the playoffs seven times while setting club records with 218 games played and 44 interceptions.

"You would have never thought this little-bitty guy could last this long in a big man's game," Green said of his longevity. "I'm proud that I have that record and proud that I've started all but two of those games. It's a record that's probably not going to be broken. When they look back 50 years from now, they'll think the record was probably held by a kicker or some big lineman. Then they'll see who it was and they'll say, 'This guy?'"

But no one who spent much time at Redskin Park was surprised.

"Darrell probably had as much to do with the success of the Redskins in the '80s and the '90s as anybody," said Richie Petitbon, Green's defensive coordinator for a decade and his coach in 1993. "He could take the best receiver out of the game with no help and enabled us to do more blitzing than normal. He's one of the best cover guys I've ever seen."

And an amazing athlete. Green's rigorous offseason conditioning helped him miss just 19 games in 16 seasons, none since 1992.

"I had talent, but I didn't sit around twiddling my thumbs," Green said. "I've prepared every day, every game, every season to try to be the best."

All that preparation paid huge dividends for the little-bitty guy and for the Redskins.

IT'S BEEN A LONG TIME

1. Which Redskin started the most consecutive games?

2. How many consecutive Redskins games did receiver Art Monk catch a pass in?

3. Which Hog played the longest for the Redskins?

4. How many of linebacker Monte Coleman's 216 games (second in club history) did he start?

5. How many seasons has cornerback Darrell Green played in every Redskins game?

6. Which Redskins defensive lineman played in the most games?

7. Which Redskins tight end played in the most games?

8. Sammy Baugh held the club record for games played for more than 20 years after he retired in 1952. How many games did Baugh play for Washington?

9. Which assistant coach spent 23 seasons with the Redskins?

10. What sideline regular can top that record with 27 seasons?

Bonus: What was so remarkable about center Len Hauss' 14-year Redskins career?

RFK STADIUM (1961-96)   *Photo courtesy of the Washington Redskins*

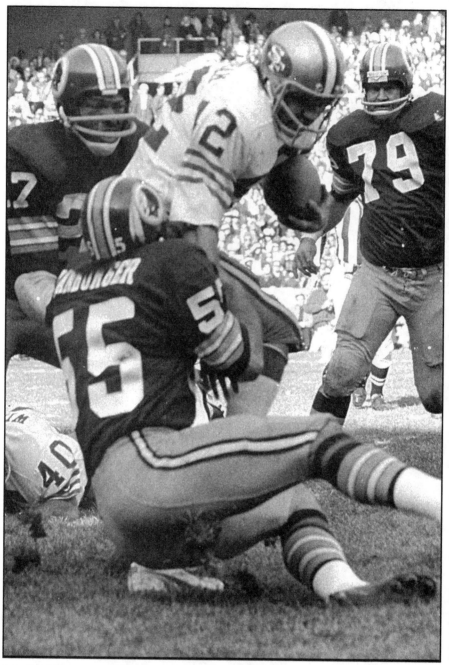

LB CHRIS HANBURGER (1965-78) *Photo courtesy of the Washington Redskins*

THE FUTURE IS NOW

BEST OF 1967-76

OFFENSE

CURT KNIGHT
K

EDDIE BROWN
KR

LARRY BROWN
RB

CHARLEY HARRAWAY
RB

SONNY JURGENSEN
QB

CHARLEY TAYLOR	JIM SNOWDEN	RAY SCHOENKE	LEN HAUSS	VINCE PROMUTO	WALT ROCK	JERRY SMITH	ROY JEFFERSON
WR	**T**	**G**	**C**	**G**	**T**	**TE**	**WR**

DEFENSE

CB	DE	DT	DT	DE	CB
PAT FISCHER	RON MCDOLE	DIRON TALBERT	BILL BRUNDIGE	VERLON BIGGS	MIKE BASS

LB	LB	LB
CHRIS HANBURGER	HAROLD MCLINTON	JACK PARDEE

S	S
KEN HOUSTON	BRIG OWENS

P	COACH
MIKE BRAGG	GEORGE ALLEN

WORKING OVERTIME

1. In the first 24 years of overtime, how many Redskins games went into the extra session?

2. What was so special about the 1990 overtime victory at Detroit?

3. How did the Redskins beat Dallas for their first overtime victory?

4. How did the Redskins lose at St. Louis for their first overtime defeat?

5. What year did the Redskins play three overtime games in four weeks?

6. How many overtime games did kicker Mark Moseley win for Washington?

7. Who scored the winning points to beat Detroit in overtime in 1995?

8. Who scored Washington's touchdown in its only overtime tie?

9. Who beat Washington with an overtime field goal in 1996?

10. What Hall of Famer dealt Washington its first overtime loss at RFK?

Bonus: What happened to Redskins rookie quarterback Heath Shuler in his first overtime game in 1994?

BRINGING THEM BACK

1. Who holds the Redskins' record for most combined returns in a season?

2. Who holds the Redskins' record for highest career kickoff return average?

3. Who holds the Redskins' record for highest kickoff return average in a season (minimum 20 returns)?

4. Who are the only two Redskins to lead the NFL in kickoff return average?

5. Who was the first Redskin to amass 1,000 yards of kickoff return yards in a season?

6. Who's the only Redskin to lead the team with an average of more than 30 yards on kickoff returns in a season?

7. This Redskin posted the lowest average kickoff return to ever lead the team. Name him.

8. Who returned a club-record 58 kickoffs in a season?

9. Name the only Redskin to return a kickoff for a touchdown during coach Joe Gibbs' 12 seasons.

10. Who was the last Redskin before Brian Mitchell (1994-97) to record 1,000 yards of kickoff returns in a season?

Bonus: Who was the last opponent to return a kickoff for a touchdown against Washington?

K MARK MOSELEY (1974-86)   *Photo courtesy of the Washington Redskins*

MARK MOSELEY

Some Redskins legends such as Sammy Baugh and Art Monk were first-round draft choices. Others such as Sonny Jurgensen and John Riggins were acquired in high-profile deals.

But Washington's alltime leading scorer became a Redskin in one of those little-noticed transactions that barely make the agate page of the sports section.

Drafted in the 14th round out of little Stephen F. Austin in 1970, Mark Moseley won Philadelphia's kicking job from veteran Sam Baker. Moseley lost his spot the next year and headed to Houston. Despite having led the AFC in field goal percentage in 1971, Moseley was cut the following September. He dug holes for septic tanks while hoping to get one more chance in the NFL.

Finally, in February 1974, Redskins coach George Allen called. Allen, unhappy with longtime kicker Curt Knight, had remembered Moseley kicking well in a 1971 downpour in Washington.

A dozen years after Allen's call, Moseley was still a Redskin, along the way becoming the first kicker to be named the league's Most Valuable Player.

"Never give up on yourself," Moseley advised when he retired in 1987 as the NFL's fourth alltime leading scorer. "If you conclude that you can play the game, don't take anyone's word that you can't."

Moseley may have missed some makeable kicks early in games, but Allen and successors Jack Pardee and Joe Gibbs knew he would always be there in the clutch. Four of Washington's first five overtime victories came on Moseley field goals. In 1981, Moseley kicked a 49-yarder on the final play to force overtime with the New York Giants and then won the game with a 48-yarder.

After nearly being waived in favor of rookie Dan Miller in 1982, Moseley opened the season by forcing overtime with a last-second 48-yarder and then beat the Eagles with a 26-yarder. Those kicks were the start of a remarkable year in which Moseley made a then-NFL-record 20 straight field goals attempts. The record-breaking 42-yarder came in the snow against the Giants with 11 seconds left and also won the game, clinching Washington's first playoff spot in six seasons.

"It was like a Hollywood script; you couldn't have written it any better," Moseley said.

He could have been describing his entire Redskins career.

LET THE POINTS SOAR

1. Who was the first Redskin to lead the NFL in scoring?

2. Name the other three Redskins to lead the NFL in scoring.

3. Washington's alltime leading scorer, Mark Moseley, played for what team after leaving the Redskins?

4. Which Redskin scored in the most consecutive games?

5. Which Redskin attempted seven field goals in a game?

6. Who kicked the longest field goal in Redskins history?

7. Which Redskin scored the most points in a game?

8. Which Redskin scored the most points in a season?

9. Which player scored the most points in a game against the Redskins?

10. Who kicked the longest field goal against the Redskins?

Bonus: Who was Moseley's holder for most of his Redskins career?

PITTED WITH PHILLY

1. What Redskins coach later coached the Eagles?

2. What Eagle recovered Gerald Riggs' fumble that set up Keith Jackson's touchdown catch which shocked the Redskins in 1989 at RFK?

3. Which Redskins rookie caught two touchdown passes (the only scores of his career) in Philadelphia in 1994?

4. Who was forced to play quarterback after the Eagles knocked Jeff Rutledge and Stan Humphries out of the "Body Bag" Game in 1990?

5. Whose crucial one-handed grab in Philadelphia helped the Redskins avenge their earlier home loss to the Eagles in 1989?

6. Who led the Eagles 81 yards in just three plays and 35 seconds to beat the Redskins in the waning moments in 1961?

7. What little-used Eagles receiver beat the eventual Super Bowl champion Redskins with a late, leaping touchdown catch in 1987?

8. What combination teamed up to pull out a last-minute Eagles victory at RFK in 1993?

9. Who scored Washington's points as the Redskins rallied from a 16-0 fourth-quarter deficit to stun the Eagles 31-28 in 1955?

10. At which of four Philadelphia stadiums have the Redskins fared best against the Eagles: Municipal Stadium, Connie Mack Stadium (formerly Shibe Park), Franklin Field or Veterans Stadium?

Bonus: Name the six ex-Redskins who played for the 1995 Eagles.

THE TRADING BLOCK

1. Whom did the Redskins trade to the Oilers for safety Ken Houston in 1973?

2. What was the price paid to the Giants for linebacker Sam Huff in 1964?

3. How did the Redskins acquire offensive tackle Jim Lachey in 1988?

4. Who was traded to Philadelphia for quarterback Sonny Jurgensen in 1964?

5. How did the Redskins acquire Cleveland running back Bobby Mitchell in 1962?

6. Name the pair of defensive tackles Washington acquired in 1990 who helped trigger a three-year playoff run.

7. What did Washington give Cleveland for running back Ernest Byner in 1989?

8. What did the trade for quarterback Joe Theismann cost the Redskins in 1974?

9. Whom did the Redskins send to New Orleans for quarterback Billy Kilmer in 1971?

10. How did the Redskins acquire 1967 Heisman Trophy-winning quarterback Gary Beban?

Bonus: Name the six "Ramskins" acquired a trade with Los Angeles by coach George Allen in 1971.

1. What three top free agents did the Redskins sign in 1976?

2. Which 1988 signee did the Redskins make the first free agent to switch teams in more than a decade?

3. Name the undrafted free agent the Redskins discovered in a mass tryout in 1972.

4. Which future four-time Pro Bowl player did the Redskins nearly cut as an undrafted free agent?

5. Which longtime starter was picked up as a free agent after being cut by Philadelphia?

6. Name the four free agents signed by the Redskins since 1992 who went on to play in a Pro Bowl.

7. What free agent pickup led the team in receiving the next three years?

8. Who were the five disappointing free agents Washington signed before the 1993 season?

9. How many former Cowboys did ex-Dallas offensive coordinator Norv Turner import during his first four seasons in Washington?

10. Who were the three Redskins who earned Super Bowl rings elsewhere after being let go by the Turner regime?

Bonus: Name the six Plan B free agent starters on Washington's 1991 Super Bowl champions.

Photo courtesy of the Washington Redskins/Scott Cunningham

COACH JOE GIBBS (1981-92)

JOE GIBBS

Vince Lombardi used fear to inspire performance and taught the Redskins how to win again. George Allen's unabashed college-like spirit made his players feel they were on a mission. But it was Joe Gibbs' low-key style that made the Redskins champions.

Lombardi and Allen were the focal points of their teams, but Gibbs was as much in the background as a head coach can be. Gibbs had what he termed a "burning desire from the time I was a young kid to compete and beat somebody," but he displayed that competitiveness with a relentless work ethic rather than with fire-and-brimstone speeches. Gibbs spent countless nights in his Redskin Park office instead of going home.

"Coach Gibbs' players were dedicated because we saw it in him," said defensive end Charles Mann, one of nine Redskins to play at least a decade for Gibbs.

"Joe Gibbs is the only coach I played for who made you feel that he would go to the wall for you," said safety Brad Edwards. "And because he made you feel that way, he got the same out of you."

What Gibbs got were three Super Bowl championships, four NFC titles and eight playoff berths in 12 seasons, the most glorious run in Washington history. Gaudy accomplishments for a former San Diego offensive coordinator who thought he might be fired by owner Jack Kent Cooke after losing his first five games during his 1981 coaching debut.

The Redskins won their first Super Bowl the following season. They returned to the title game the next year and won it again in 1987 and 1991. Only Gibbs captured Super Bowls with three different quarterbacks (Joe Theismann, Doug Williams and Mark Rypien). And Gibbs guided Washington to the NFC Championship game with a fourth passer (Jay Schroeder). Gibbs' career record of 140-65 ranks third alltime.

With nothing left to prove, an exhausted Gibbs retired from the Redskins at 52 in 1993 with his place in the Hall of Fame assured. Washington, which hadn't made the playoffs for four years before Gibbs' arrival, missed them in the five seasons following his departure. Those facts only emphasized the humble Gibbs' role in the Redskins' success.

HE'S THE BOSS

1. Name the only Redskins coach with a perfect home record in the playoffs.

2. What was so special about Vince Lombardi's one season as Washington's coach?

3. Who was Washington's least successful coach?

4. Which coach holds the club record for winning percentage?

5. Which coach was part of all five of Washington's Super Bowl teams?

6. Who had a better record against Dallas, George Allen or Joe Gibbs?

7. Which team did Gibbs beat for his first victory after an 0-5 start in his 1981 debut?

8. Who's the only Redskins' coach besides Gibbs and Allen to win 50 games in Washington?

9. How many future NFL coaches were assistants for the 1972 Redskins?

10. Who coached the Redskins in 1970, the season between Lombardi's death and Allen's arrival?

Bonus: How many times since 1945 have the Redskins made the playoffs with a Democrat in the White House?

CLASHING WITH THE CARDS

1. Which great Cardinals quarterback finished his career with the Redskins?

2. What did Washington have to give St. Louis as compensation for signing free agent defensive tackle Dave Butz in 1975?

3. What former Cardinals head coach was on Washington's staff for Super Bowl XXVI in 1991?

4. What position did Joe Gibbs hold in St. Louis from 1973-77?

5. What former Redskins quarterback led the Cardinals to a victory over Washington in 1994?

6. What did the Redskins give the Cardinals after signing free agent cornerback Pat Fischer in 1968?

7. What ex-St. Louis star runner finished his career with the Redskins in 1981?

8. Who picked off three Cardinals passes to lead the Redskins to victory in their first game under coach George Allen in 1971?

9. What did Redskins quarterback Sammy Baugh do against the Cardinals on "Sammy Baugh Day" in 1947?

10. Whose 71-yard punt return on Monday Night Football during monsoon-like conditions at RFK helped the Redskins sweep the Cardinals in 1976?

Bonus: Against which version of the Cardinals have the Redskins had the most success: Chicago, St. Louis or Phoenix-Arizona?

G RUSS GRIMM (1981-91) *Photo courtesy of the Washington Redskins/Scott Cunningham*

BACK ON TOP

BEST OF 1977-86

OFFENSE

MARK MOSELEY
K

MIKE NELMS
KR

JOHN RIGGINS
RB

JOE WASHINGTON
RB

JOE THEISMANN
QB

ART MONK	JOE JACOBY	RUSS GRIMM	JEFF BOSTIC	MARK MAY	GEORGE STARKE	DON WARREN	CHARLIE BROWN
WR	**T**	**G**	**C**	**G**	**T**	**TE**	**WR**

DEFENSE

CB	**DE**	**DT**	**DT**	**DE**	**CB**
JOE LAVENDER	DEXTER MANLEY	DAVE BUTZ	DARRYL GRANT	CHARLES MANN	LEMAR PARRISH

LB	**LB**	**LB**
BRAD DUSEK	NEAL OLKEWICZ	RICH MILOT

S	**S**
MARK MURPHY	TONY PETERS

P	**COACH**
MIKE BRAGG	JOE GIBBS

RB JOHN RIGGINS (1976-79, 81-85)   *Photo courtesy of the Washington Redskins*

JOHN RIGGINS

If John Riggins hadn't insisted on a no-trade clause in order to return to the Redskins in 1981, he might not be in the Hall of Fame and there might be one fewer Super Bowl trophy on display at Jack Kent Cooke Stadium.

The ever-eccentric Riggins, who had worn his hair in an Afro and a Mohawk while playing for the New York Jets before coming to the Redskins as a free agent in 1976, had walked away after leading Washington within a whisker of the playoffs in 1979.

When new coach Joe Gibbs left his first meeting with Riggins in 1981, he thought his holdout running back was "a fruitcake." Gibbs decided to trade Riggins as soon as he returned. But when Riggins agreed to come back, it was only with a no-trade clause added to his contract.

A year later, Riggins told Gibbs to "give me the football, baby," and proceeded to rumble through postseason like no runner in NFL history. The 33-year-old Riggins gained over 100 yards in a record four straight playoff games en route to a total of 610.

Deceptively fast for a 6-foot-2, 240-pound back, Riggins running behind the young offensive line nicknamed "the Hogs" was an irrestible force. If Washington had the lead in the fourth quarter, Gibbs would go to the "Riggo Drill," feeding Riggins the ball over and over as exhausted defenders were strewn like so many bowling pins.

"Riggins just came blowing by us all day," lamented Minnesota linebacker Scott Studwell after Riggins had run for a career-high 185 yards in a 1982 playoff victory over the Vikings.

Riggins bowed to the RFK Stadium crowd after that performance. Late in the NFC Championship Game victory over Dallas the next week, Gibbs ran Riggins up the middle on nine straight plays. And Riggins' 43-yard touchdown burst in the fourth quarter of Super Bowl XVII against Miami sewed up Washington's first championship in 40 years.

The following season, Riggins set a then-NFL record with 24 touchdowns while rushing for what was then a club-best 1,347 yards and helping the Redskins defend their NFC title.

When he retired for good in 1985, Riggins was the NFL's fourth alltime leading rusher and the only runner in the top 20 to gain more yards after his 30th birthday than beforehand. But then Riggins was never one to take the conventional path.

ON THE RUN

1. Which Redskin has rushed for the most yards in a season?

2. Who was the first Redskin to lead the NFL in rushing?

3. Three Redskins rushed for 1,000 yards in a season in the 1970s. John Riggins and Larry Brown were two. Name the third.

4. Who led the Redskins in rushing in 1980, the year Riggins held out?

5. Who averaged a club-record 5.42 yards in a season (with at least 100 carries)?

6. Who holds the club record for 100-yard games in a season?

7. Which Redskin has the highest career rushing average with at least 250 carries?

8. Who holds the club record for carries in a game?

9. Who holds the club record for rushing yards in a game?

10. Which opponent carried a record 36 times against Washington?

Bonus: Who has rushed for the most yards in a game against Washington?

PLAYOFF TIME

1. Who dropped a sure Redskins touchdown early in the record-setting 73-0 loss to Chicago in the 1940 NFL Championship Game?

2. Which Bear did Darrell Green hurdle en route to his 52-yard punt return touchdown that beat Chicago in the 1987 playoffs?

3. Which defensive lineman did coach George Allen make a starter in a 5-2 scheme to shut down Green Bay's powerful running attack in 1972?

4. Who was the only quarterback to beat the Redskins in a playoff game at RFK?

5. Who was the receiver who came out of nowhere to catch three touchdown passes in a 1982 playoff game?

6. Which Redskins defensive lineman had three sacks in the team's last playoff victory for coach Joe Gibbs?

7. Who threw the pass that Minnesota's Darrin Nelson couldn't hold on the final play of the 1987 NFC Championship Game?

8. Which Redskin had an interception in each of the team's three playoff victories (including the Super Bowl) in 1991?

9. The Redskins lost to the Los Angeles Rams 19-10 in a 1974 playoff game that was Sonny Jurgensen's last NFL contest. Who scored Washington's points?

10. Why did Billy Kilmer almost miss the 1973 playoff game at Minnesota?

Bonus: The Redskins have met 14 teams in postseason. Which one have they never beaten?

Photo courtesy of the Washington Redskins/Scott Cunningham

DE CHARLES MANN (1983-93)

AN END TO AN ERA
BEST OF 1987-97

OFFENSE

CHIP LOHMILLER
(K)

BRIAN MITCHELL
(KR)

EARNEST BYNER
(RB)

TERRY ALLEN
(RB)

MARK RYPIEN
(QB)

ART MONK	JIM LACHEY	RALEIGH MCKENZIE	JEFF BOSTIC	MARK SCHLERETH	ED SIMMONS	DON WARREN	GARY CLARK
(WR)	(T)	(G)	(C)	(G)	(T)	(TE)	(WR)

DEFENSE

CB	DE	DT	DT	DE	CB
DARRELL GREEN	DEXTER MANLEY	TIM JOHNSON	ERIC WILLIAMS	CHARLES MANN	TOM CARTER

LB	LB	LB
KEN HARVEY	WILBUR MARSHALL	ANDRE COLLINS

S	S
BRAD EDWARDS	ALVIN WALTON

P
MATT TURK

COACH
JOE GIBBS

KR BRIAN MITCHELL (1990-) *Photo courtesy of the Washington Redskins/Bill Wood*

BRIAN MITCHELL

As the first player in NCAA history to pass for over 5,000 yards and run for over 3,000 yards during his career, Brian Mitchell didn't leave Southwestern Louisiana with the intention of being a kick returner in the NFL. And through eight seasons with the Redskins, Mitchell has stubbornly refused to be labeled as such. But despite a famous stint as the emergency quarterback as a rookie in 1990 and despite rushing for over 100 yards off the bench in Joe Gibbs' final victory in 1992 and as a starter in Richie Petibon's 1993 debut, Mitchell has been most valuable returning kicks.

In 1994, Mitchell set an NFL record with 1,930 yards worth of combined returns. The following year, he was the NFC's Pro Bowl kick returner, following in the steps of such Redskins as Herb Mul-Key, Eddie Brown, Tony Green and Mike Nelms. Mitchell's 12.4-yard punt return average from 1994-97 was the league's best. Mitchell is second in NFL history in kickoff return yards and combined return yards and his eight return touchdowns rank fourth.

"Brian's one of the best returners in the NFL," said Pete Rodriguez, Mitchell's special teams coach from 1994-97. "He has great quickness, excellent instincts and tremendous toughness."

That toughness hasn't earned Mitchell many friends on opposing teams. His willingness to run over instead of around tacklers and his penchant for yapping at punters and special teams coaches who won't kick to him have likely limited his Pro Bowl votes.

Mitchell is proudest of his versatility. Not only does he return both punts *and* kickoffs unlike 1996-97 NFC Pro Bowl return specialist Michael Bates, but Mitchell is a very talented third-down back. From 1993-96, Mitchell was Washington's second-leading rusher and in 1995, its second-leading receiver.

Put all those skills together and Mitchell led the NFL in combined yards from 1994-96. The only other players to do so three straight years were Hall of Famers Jim Brown and Gale Sayers. And only an amazing season by Detroit superstar Barry Sanders stopped Mitchell's streak in 1997.

"I've never been one to limit myself," Mitchell likes to say. "I'm not a kick returner or a running back. I'm a football player."

A supremely gifted one.

MANY HAPPY RETURNS

1. Which Redskin set an NFL record by returning 11 punts in a game?

2. Who holds the Redskins' record for highest punt return average in a season and a career?

3. Who led Washington in punt returns in 1974?

4. Who's the only Redskin besides Brian Mitchell to lead the team in punt returns for six straight seasons?

5. Which Redskin led the team with a 0.7 yard punt return average?

6. Mitchell returned two punts for touchdowns in 1991 and 1994. Name the other three Redskins to match that feat.

7. How did Mitchell debut as Washington's regular punt returner?

8. Who was the last player to return a punt for a touchdown against Washington?

9. Which Redskin returned a club-record 57 punts in a season?

10. Who holds the club record for highest punt return average in a season?

Bonus: Name the four Redskins besides Mitchell to lead the NFL in punt return average.

THE BIG PLAYS

1. Who holds the Redskins' record for the longest run?

2. Who holds the Redskins' record for the longest interception return?

3. Which Redskin returned a kickoff 95 yards but didn't score?

4. Who holds the Redskins' record for the longest punt return?

5. What's the longest kickoff return in a Washington game?

6. Who holds the Redskins' record for the longest fumble return?

7. Who holds the Redskins' record for the longest kickoff return?

8. Who teamed up for the only 99-yard completion against the Redskins?

9. Who holds the record for the longest run against Washington?

10. Who had the longest punt return against the Redskins?

Bonus: Name the three combinations who hooked up for 99-yard pass plays for the Redskins.

AT THE TOP

1. Who was Washington's first draft pick?

2. What was so odd about 1968 first-rounder Jim "Yazoo" Smith?

3. Who was Mike Sommer?

4. What do I.B. Hale and Andre Johnson have in common?

5. Who was Washington's only first-rounder from a non-Division I school?

6. Who was the last running back taken by Washington in the first round?

7. Did the Redskins ever use their top pick on a kicker?

8. Who was the last local college player drafted by Washington in the first round?

9. Name the all-American quarterback from Maryland and subsequent Redskins first-rounder who bombed as Sammy Baugh's replacement.

10. Name the only Pro Bowl offensive lineman the Redskins ever took in the first round.

Bonus: Whom did the Redskins draft twice in the first round?

THE LATER ROUNDS

1. Name the 11th-round draft choice who played during four presidencies in Washington.

2. What Redskin took just three seasons to go from the 10th round to the Pro Bowl?

3. Which college basketball star did the Redskins draft in 1976?

4. George Allen was famous for trading draft picks, but four of his choices became Washington regulars. Name them.

5. Which Olympian did the Redskins draft in 1953?

6. Which future national championship coach did Washington choose in 1956?

7. Which nine-time Pro Bowl star was an 18th-round Redskin pick?

8. What NFL Most Valuable Player was a Redskins "future" selection in 1945?

9. What was so remarkable about coach Joe Gibbs' first draft in 1981?

10. Who were the only players drafted by Washington before 1994 to play for the 1997 Redskins?

Bonus: What Redskins draft produced two Hall of Famers?

DE DEXTER MANLEY (1981-89)   *Photo courtesy of the Washington Redskins*

DEXTER MANLEY

Defensive end Dexter Manley won a game for the Redskins by prompting a penalty on a guard into whose face he had spit or, as he kiddingly put it, "sneezed." Manley once memorably mixed his metaphors when threatening San Francisco quarterback Joe Montana, vowing to "ring his clock." Another time, Manley sported a Mohawk haircut and started calling himself "Mr. D" as in defense.

"Dexter was always fun to be around," said Charles Mann, the other defensive end for the Redskins during the final seven of Manley's nine seasons in Washington.

"I'll always remember Dexter's enthusiasm," said Redskins general manager Charley Casserly. "He loved everything about being a football player: the games, the practices, working out."

However, Manley could infuriate opponents with his brash statements. Chicago coach Mike Ditka once accused him of having "the IQ of a grapefruit." But Manley also had a sensitive side, emotionally confessing to a congressional committee that he had never learned to read although he had attended Oklahoma State for five years.

Wild-eyed or teary-eyed, Manley could always get to the quarterback. The Redskins' record book tells the story: most sacks, career, Manley, 97.5; most sacks, season, Manley, 18; most sacks, game, Manley, four. From 1984-86, Manley *averaged* 15.5 sacks. No other Redskin has had that many in any season.

Manley's sack knocked Dallas quarterback Danny White out of the 1982 NFC Championship Game and he then tipped a pass by backup Gary Hogeboom which Darryl Grant intercepted for the touchdown which clinched Washington's first Super Bowl trip in 10 years.

"Dexter could throw [massive offensive tackle] Joe Jacoby around like a rag doll in practice," Mann said. "Dexter had so much God-given talent, the strength, the speed, the quickness."

However in 1989, Manley was suspended for a year after his third positive drug test. He was just 30. He never played for the Redskins again. Manley resurfaced with Phoenix and Tampa Bay before another positive test in 1991 left him watching on television as his former teammates won the Super Bowl, their first without him.

"I felt very envious watching [the game]," said Manley, who closed out his career with Ottawa of the Canadian Football League in 1992. "I thought to myself, 'Look what drugs took away from me.'"

SAC-K-INGS

1. Who's the Redskins' career leader in sacks?

2. What's the team record for sacks in a game?

3. What's the fewest sacks the Redskins allowed in a season?

4. Who recorded the last Redskins' sack at RFK?

5. Who recorded the last opposition sack at RFK?

6. Who recorded the first Redskins' sack at Cooke Stadium?

7. Who recorded the first opposition sack at Cooke Stadium?

8. Name the two Redskins to record four sacks in a game.

9. Who holds the Redskins' record for career sacks by a linebacker?

10. Who was the last defensive back to record a sack at RFK?

Bonus: Name the six Redskins to total at least 13 sacks in a season.

THE SUPER BOWLS

1. Who scored Washington's lone touchdown in Super Bowl VII?

2. Who was Joe Theismann throwing to on the "Rocket Screen" which the Raiders' Jack Squirek picked off and returned for a touchdown in Super Bowl XVIII?

3. Which Dolphin did John Riggins bounce off on the way to his game-winning touchdown in Super Bowl XVII?

4. Which Redskin had two sacks in Super Bowl XXII?

5. Which Redskin intercepted two passes in Super Bowl XXVI?

6. Which Redskin has scored the most points in Super Bowls?

7. Whose fumble recovery helped turn Super Bowl XXII in Washington's favor after Denver had jumped on top 10-0?

8. Who scored Washington's first offensive Super Bowl touchdown?

9. Joe Theismann dived to break up an interception in Super Bowl XVII. Who was the Dolphin who almost made the play?

10. Which Redskins starters in Super Bowl VII had previous Super Bowl experience?

Bonus: Which Redskin has caught the most passes in Super Bowls?

**COACH JOE GIBBS (1981-92) &
QB JOE THEISMANN (1974-85)**

Photo courtesy of the Washington Redskins

THE ANSWERS

PASSING FANCY

1. Jay Schroeder with 4,109 in 1986.

2. John Friesz against the Giants in 1994.

3. Joe Theismann with 2,044.

4. Sammy Baugh with 446 against the Boston Yanks in 1948.

5. Mark Rypien against Atlanta in 1991.

6. Norm Snead with 27 in 1963.

7. Sonny Jurgensen with 58 percent.

8. Arizona's Boomer Esiason with 522 yards in 1996.

9. Philadelphia's Adrian Burk in 1954 and the Giants' Y.A. Tittle in 1962.

10. Philadelphia's Davy O'Brien with 60 in a 1940 game.

Bonus: Eddie LeBaron in 1958.

THE NICKNAMES

1. Ron McDole.

2. Charley Justice.

3. John "The Diesel" Riggins.

4. Billy Kilmer.

5. Turk Edwards.

6. "Bullet" Bill Dudley.

7. Leslie "Speedy" Duncan.

8. Lionel Vital.

9. Mark Schlereth.

10. Hugh Taylor.

Bonus: Christian Adolph Jurgensen.

THE HALL OF FAMERS

1. David "Deacon" Jones.

2. Four: Ray Flaherty, Curly Lambeau, Vince Lombardi and Joe Gibbs. Lambeau and Lombardi were elected for their accomplishments in Green Bay.

3. Owner George Preston Marshall and quarterback Sammy Baugh were charter enshrinees in 1963.

4. Twenty with the 1998 election of safety Paul Krause.

5. Six: Marshall, Flaherty, Baugh, running back Cliff Battles receiver Wayne Millner and tackle Albert "Turk" Edwards.

6. Bill Dudley in 1953, Sam Huff in 1969 and John Riggins in 1980.

7. San Diego, where he had been the offensive coordinator.

8. Otto Graham, a star for Cleveland, was 17-22-3 as Washington's coach from 1966-68.

9. Stan Jones.

10. Receiver Charley Taylor, 165.

Bonus: Sammy Baugh (1937-52), Taylor (1964-77) and Gibbs (1981-93).

WELCOME TO WASHINGTON

1. Boston. They were the Braves in 1932 before becoming the Redskins the following season.

2. Halfback Cliff Battles from West Virginia Wesleyan and tackle Albert "Turk" Edwards from Washington State. Each is enshrined in the Pro Football Hall of Fame.

3. Braves Field, home of baseball's Boston Braves. The team moved to Fenway Park, home of the Red Sox in 1933.

4. Frustrated by a lack of support (the final two crowds at Fenway were under 5,000) and a lack of press coverage, Marshall switched the 1936 NFL Championship Game to New York's Polo Grounds and then moved his franchise to Washington.

5. Riley Smith with a pair of 18-yard field goals and an extra point after his 60-yard touchdown jaunt with an interception as the Redskins beat the Giants 13-3 on Sept. 15, 1937.

6. Clark Griffith, the owner of baseball's Senators, an American League franchise from 1901-71 until it moved to Arlington, Texas.

7. The Senators, named after their baseball counterparts, lasted for just the 1921 season.

8. Ten. They were 53-17-3 at home during their first decade at Griffith. They would manage just two more winning home records in their final 14 seasons on Georgia Avenue.

9. Two. The 73-0 debacle against Chicago in 1940 and the 14-6 revenge victory over the Bears two years later. The defense picked off three Sid Luckman passes. Sammy Baugh's 38-yard touchdown throw to Wilbur Moore and Andy Farkas' 1-yard run provided enough points for the championship.

10. The expansion Dallas Cowboys, 26-14, on Oct. 9, 1960.

Bonus: 35,540

JUST FOR KICKS

1. Sammy Baugh with 14 against Philadelphia in 1939.

2. Steve Cox, Greg Coleman, Tommy Barnhardt and Chip Lohmiller.

3. Jeff Hayes.

4. Mike Bragg (1977), Hayes (1983) and Matt Turk (1995).

5. Baugh against Detroit in 1940.

6. Sam Baker with a 45.2-yard average in 1958.

7. Dick Poillon.

8. Pat Richter with 91 in 1964.

9. Kelly Goodburn.

10. Steve Cox booted a 77-yarder against Buffalo in 1987.

Bonus: Eddie LeBaron in 1952, 1953 and 1955.

GRAPPLING WITH THE GIANTS

1. Snapper John Brandes. The Redskins maintained that the Giants only claimed Brandes off waivers (which he had to pass through to be activated off injured reserve) to raid their playbook for the game two days later at Giants Stadium. The Redskins won anyway, 28-10. Brandes' Giants career lasted one month.

2. Jurgensen tore his Achilles' tendon and was lost for the season, the only year of his 11 in Washington that the Redskins played for the championship.

3. Angry, intoxicated Giants fans showered Brown with beer as he left the field after rushing for 191 yards in Washington's 23-16 victory.

4. Referee Bill Halloran ruled that the field goal try by Washington's Bo Russell was wide right. New York won 9-7 despite a tirade Redskins coach Ray Flaherty directed at Halloran.

5. The Redskins won 21-7 at home the following September thanks in part to a 78-yard punt return by Dick Todd.

6. Schroeder hit receiver Art Monk for a 44-yard gain and wound up rallying the Redskins to a 23-21 victory. Theismann never played again.

7. Battles scored on runs of 75 and 76 yards.

8. Raul Allegre.

9. Rookie safety Brig Owens.

10. Fullback Max Krause.

Bonus: The Redskins were shut out for the only time in Gibbs' 12 seasons and they lost an NFC Championship Game for the only time in his five tries as the Giants won 17-0 at the icy, windy Meadowlands.

THE FRONT OFFICE

1. A sometime theater producer, Marshall made his money as the owner of the Palace Laundry chain.

2. Marshall's second wife, former silent movie actress Corinne Griffith, wrote the words. Washington bandleader Barnee Breskin wrote the music. The song debuted in 1938 along with the NFL's first marching band.

3. Nine. Dutch Bergman (1943), Dud DeGroot (1944-45), Turk Edwards (1946-48), John Whelchel (1949), Herman Ball (1949-51), Dick Todd (1951), Curly Lambeau (1952-53), Joe Kuharich (1954-58) and Mike Nixon (1959-60) were all found wanting. Marshall replaced Nixon with Bill McPeak but wasn't in charge when the coach was let go in favor of Otto Graham after the 1965 season.

4. "I gave him an unlimited budget and he exceeded it."

5. Former Miami player personnel director Bobby Beathard became Washington's GM. Jack Pardee came from Chicago, where he had been coaching the Bears, to accept a similar role with his old team.

6. Baseball's Baltimore Orioles.

7. The NBA's Los Angeles Lakers and the NHL's Los Angeles Kings.

8. It ended in 1979 with a world-record divorce settlement of $49 million to the former Jeanne Carnegie.

9. Beathard was a studio analyst for NBC for a year before becoming San Diego's GM in 1990.

10. He was hired as an unpaid 28-year-old intern by Allen in 1977.

Bonus: The District (next to RFK), Potomac Yards (Alexandria, Va.) and Laurel, Md.

THE REST OF THE LEAGUE

1. The Los Angeles Rams, 51-7 in 1983.

2. Arizona, Carolina, New Orleans and Tampa Bay.

3. Green Bay.

4. Baltimore (formerly Cleveland). The Redskins have never visited three-year NFL franchise Jacksonville.

5. San Diego is 0-5 against Washington.

6. The New York Jets beat the Redskins 3-0 in 1993.

7. Chicago. The Redskins are 4-3 against the Bears in the playoffs.

8. The Colts won 12 of the 15 matchups from 1953-67.

9. Pittsburgh, 73 times. Washington leads the series 42-28-3.

10. The Redskins are 0-4 at the Oilers and 0-3 at Kansas City, Miami and the Raiders.

Bonus: Washington was the only NFL team to go 3-0 against the Jaguars and Panthers during their first three seasons.

PRO BOWL PICKS

1. Running back Bill Dudley, quarterback Harry Gilmer and tackle Paul Lipscomb.

2. Linebacker Chris Hanburger (1966-69, 1972-76).

3. Defensive end Gene Brito (1953, 1955-58).

4. 1993.

5. Linebacker Ken Harvey (1994-97).

6. 1991. They were quarterback Mark Rypien, running back Earnest Byner, receiver Gary Clark, offensive tackle Jim Lachey, guard Mark Schlereth, defensive end Charles Mann, cornerback Darrell Green and kicker Chip Lohmiller.

7. Hall of Fame safety Ken Houston (1973-78).

8. Charley Taylor was chosen as a running back in 1964-65 and as a receiver in 1966-67 and 1972-75.

9. Florida kick returner Tony Green in 1978.

10. 1986, after their NFC Championship Game loss to the Giants.

Bonus: Kick returners Eddie Brown (1976-77) and Mike Nelms (1980-81), kicker Mark Moseley (1979 and 1982) and punter Matt Turk (1996-97).

PICKING THEM OFF

1. Don Sandifer with 13 in 1948.

2. Sammy Baugh against Detroit in 1943 and Sandifer against the Boston Yanks in 1948.

3. Hall of Famer Paul Krause in 1964.

4. Brig Owens with 686.

5. Andre Collins.

6. Philadelphia's Randall Cunningham, four times (once in the playoffs).

7. San Diego's Ed Luther in 1983.

8. Pittsburgh's Jack Butler in 1953 and Jerry Norton of the St. Louis Cardinals in 1960.

9. Phoenix's Robert Massey in 1992.

10. Mark Murphy with nine in 1983 and Barry Wilburn with nine in 1987.

Bonus: Sandifer (1948), Dale Hackbart (1961), Vernon Dean (1984) and Collins (1994).

FIGHT FOR OLD D.C.

1. The $24 million stadium was built by the federal government. A crowd of 36,767 was on hand for the Oct. 1, 1961 opener against the Giants. The Redskins blew a 21-7 lead and lost 24-21.

2. Washington's Jim Kerr fumbled the opening kickoff. New York's Pat Summerall, who had kicked the ball, recovered the fumble.

3. Giants receiver Kyle Rote on a 17-yard pass from quarterback Charlie Conerly.

4. Running back Don Boessler on a 3-yard pass from quarterback Norm Snead.

5. Cornerback Dale Hackbart.

6. Giants quarterback Y.A. Tittle.

7. Eight games. They beat the Cowboys 34-24 on Dec. 17 in the 1961 season finale to snap a 23-game winless streak.

8. Halfback Dick James set a Redskins record by scoring four touchdowns.

9. Bill McPeak. McPeak debuted at 1-12-1 that season and was 21 games under .500 in his first three seasons. With the additions of Sonny Jurgensen, Charley Taylor and Sam Huff in 1964, the Redskins improved. They went 6-8 that season and in 1965, but McPeak was still fired and replaced by Otto Graham.

10. Nine.

Bonus: In 1969, a year after Senator Robert F. Kennedy, the presidential candidate and former Attorney General, was assassinated.

IT'S BETTER TO RECEIVE

1. Anthony Allen caught 257 yards of passes in a 1987 replacement game against the St. Louis Cardinals.

2. Bobby Mitchell with 1,436 in 1963.

3. Bones Taylor (1952), Charley Taylor (1966), Jerry Smith (1967) and Ricky Sanders (1988).

4. Charley Taylor (1964-77) with 79.

5. Ricky Sanders caught 80 passes in 1989.

6. Gary Clark and Art Monk.

7. Philadelphia's Don Looney caught 14 passes against Washington in 1940.

8. Bob Shaw of the Los Angeles Rams in 1949.

9. Halfback Joe Washington with 70 catches in 1981.

10. Del Shofner of the New York Giants hauled in 269 yards on 11 catches against Washington in a 1962 game.

Bonus: Monk caught 13 passes against Cincinnati in 1985 and against Detroit in 1990. Halfback Kelvin Bryant caught 13 against the Giants in 1986.

DUELING WITH DALLAS

1. Ex-Redskin Eddie LeBaron.

2. Landry was 32-24-2 against Washington. Johnson was 5-5.

3. Receiver Tony Hill on the last regular season touchdown pass of Hall of Famer Roger Staubach's career.

4. Safety Brig Owens (whose career began on the Dallas taxi squad in 1965) on a 26-yard interception return and receiver Charley Taylor on a 1-yard pass from quarterback Sonny Jurgensen.

5. They dressed in battle fatigues for the trip to Texas since they felt they were going to war. They won 34-14.

6. Receiver Teddy Wilson on a 16-yard reverse.

7. Defensive tackle Jason Buck forced the fumble. After a wild scramble, safety Danny Copeland recovered it in the end zone for a touchdown and the 20-17 victory.

8. Receiver Angelo Coia on a 5-yard pass from Jurgensen.

9. Nickel back Ken Stone.

10. Guard John Wilbur played for Dallas from 1966-69.

Bonus: Cowboys running back Robert Newhouse. Redskins offensive tackle George Starke, a starter in 1982, was on the taxi squad in 1972.

1. Dallas running back Herschel Walker.

2. Running back Stephen Davis.

3. Quarterback Gus Frerotte and tight end Jamie Asher against San Francisco on Nov. 24.

4. Washington's Henry Ellard to become just the second 35 year-old receiver to surpass 1,000 yards in a season.

5. Walker, who was tackled by Redskins linebacker Ken Harvey.

6. Cowboys safety George Teague.

7. Redskins fullback Larry Bowie for an illegal block.

8. Simmons rushed back from five weeks on the inactive list to play in the meaningless final game at RFK as a cap to his first 10 years as a Redskin.

9. San Francisco won the penultimate game at RFK, 19-16 in overtime, on Nov. 24, 1996.

10. Cleveland (8-2), the Raiders (3-2) and Seattle (3-2).

Bonus: George Allen (40-10-1).

HELLO TO RALJON

1. Washington kick returner Brian Mitchell.

2. Washington kicker Scott Blanton.

3. Arizona's Tommy Bennett scored after teammate J.J. McCleskey blocked Matt Turk's punt, the first such miscue suffered by the Redskins in more than five years.

4. Redskins receiver Michael Westbrook.

5. Redskins running back Stephen Davis.

6. Baltimore on Oct. 26, 1997.

7. Arizona linebacker Ronald McKinnon.

8. The Redskins beat the Cowboys 21-16 on Oct. 13, 1997.

9. It was forced by Cris Dishman and recovered by fellow Redskins cornerback Darryl Pounds.

10. Dallas linebacker Dexter Coakley.

Bonus: Washington, D.C. (1937): Ballston, Va. (1938); Spokane, Wash. (1939-40); San Diego (1941-44); Georgetown U. (1945); Occidental College, Los Angeles (1946-62); Dickinson College, Carlisle, Pa. (1963-94).

IT'S BEEN A LONG TIME

1. Center Len Hauss started 192 in a row.

2. 164 for Washington, 183 overall.

3. Center Jeff Bostic played 184 games over 14 seasons.

4. Just 62.

5. Ten, including the past five.

6. Dave Butz, 203.

7. Don Warren, 194.

8. 137.

9. LaVern "Torgy" Torgeson was a Redskins assistant from 1959-61, 1971-77 and 1981-93. Torgeson also played with Washington from 1955-58.

10. Trainer Bubba Tyer has been with the Redskins since 1971.

Bonus: Hauss never missed a game, playing in 196 straight.

WORKING OVERTIME

1. The Redskins are 11-7-1 in overtime (6-4-1 at home and 5-3 on the road). They played overtime in 1975, 1976, 1978, 1981, 1982, 1986, 1987, 1988, 1990, 1994, 1995, 1996 and 1997.

2. Chip Lohmiller's game-winning field goal capped the greatest comeback in team history. The Redskins trailed by 21 points in the third quarter and 14 points in the fourth before rallying behind backup quarterback Jeff Rutledge to win 41-38.

3. Safety Ken Houston picked off a pass by fellow Hall of Famer Roger Staubach setting up the game-winning sneak by 36-year-old quarterback Billy Kilmer. Washington 30, Dallas 24 on Nov. 2, 1975.

4. The officials ruled Cardinals receiver Mel Gray's juggling act at the goal line against cornerback Pat Fischer was a touchdown, tying the game with 20 seconds left. Jim Bakken's field goal won it in overtime, 20-17 on Nov. 16, 1975, helping to knock the Redskins from the playoffs for the first time in five years under coach George Allen.

5. 1975. In addition to the aforementioned Dallas and St. Louis games, Washington lost 26-23 to Oakland on Nov. 23 at RFK.

6. Four. Moseley beat the Giants in 1978 at home and in 1981 on the road and the Eagles in 1976 and 1982 in Philadelphia.

7. Cornerback Darrell Green picked off a pass by Scott Mitchell and returned it seven yards for the winning touchdown.

8. Quarterback Gus Frerotte ran the ball over to give Washington a 7-0 lead in 1997 against the Giants. But Frerotte had to leave the game with a sprained neck after head-butting an end zone retaining wall in celebration. The game finished in a 7-7 tie.

9. Arizona's Kevin Butler. The Cardinals, who trailed 34-20 in the fourth quarter, won 37-34, in a wild game that featured five field goal attempts in overtime.

10. Oakland kicker George Blanda with a 27-yard field goal.

Bonus: Shuler, the third pick in the draft, threw five interceptions in a 19-16 loss to Arizona and sprained his ankle, losing his job for the first of three times to Frerotte.

BRINGING THEM BACK

1. Larry Jones with an NFL-record 100 in 1975.

2. Bobby Mitchell with a 28.5-yard average.

3. Mike Nelms with a 29.7-yard average in 1981.

4. Nelms in 1981 and Eddie Saenz in 1947.

5. Herb Mul-Key with 1,011 yards in 1973.

6. Andy Farkas averaged 51.5 yards on four returns in 1942.

7. Keith Griffin averaged 19.1 yards in 1987.

8. Brian Mitchell in 1994.

9. Joe Howard Johnson went 99 yards against the Raiders in 1989.

10. Ken Jenkins with 1,018 yards in 1985.

Bonus: Thomas Lewis of the New York Giants took one back 90 yards for a touchdown against the Redskins in 1995.

LET THE POINTS SOAR

1. Andy Farkas led the league with 68 points in 1939.

2. Sam Baker (1957), Mark Moseley (1983) and Chip Lohmiller (1991).

3. Cleveland in 1986.

4. Chip Lohmiller scored in 92 straight games from Sept. 1988-Dec. 1993.

5. Curt Knight tried seven field goals vs. Houston in 1971. He set the club record (since equalled six times) by making five.

6. Steve Cox, usually a punter, kicked a 57-yarder against Seattle in 1986.

7. Running backs Dick James (vs. Dallas in 1961) and Larry Brown (vs. Philadelphia in 1973) each scored 24 points in a game.

8. Moseley scored 161 points in 1983 while also setting club records with 62 extra points and 33 field goals.

9. Chicago Cardinals receiver/kicker Bobby Joe Conrad scored 25 points against Washington in 1959.

10. Kansas City's Nick Lowery kicked a 58-yarder against Washington in 1983. Ironically, Lowery was a graduate of Washington's St. Albans School.

Bonus: Joe Theismann.

PITTED WITH PHILLY

1. Joe Kuharich coached in Washington from 1954-58 and in Philadelphia from 1964-68.

2. Defensive end Al Harris recovered the ball and lateraled to safety Wes Hopkins, who dashed 77 yards to the Washington 4. Jackson scored shortly thereafter to complete Philadelphia's comeback from a late 37-28 deficit to win 42-37.

3. Receiver Tydus Winans on a pair of throws from fellow rookie Heath Shuler.

4. Rookie running back Brian Mitchell, who had been a record-setting option quarterback at Southwestern Louisiana.

5. Tight end Jimmie Johnson, a rookie from Howard University.

6. Quarterback Sonny Jurgensen to complete a 413-yard afternoon. Jurgensen would be traded to Washington three years later.

7. Gregg Garrity.

8. Quarterback Bubby Brister hit fullback James Joseph with a 2-yard touchdown pass with 46 seconds left to win 17-14.

9. Halfback Vic Janowicz scored two touchdowns, a field goal and four extra points. Ralph Thomas recovered Jerry Norton's fumbled kickoff return for a touchdown and quarterback Eddie LeBaron took the ball over on a sneak as the Redskins scored 31 points in the fourth quarter.

10. The Redskins were 3-0 at Municipal. They were 6-9-3 at Shibe/Connie Mack and 8-6 at Franklin. They're 13-14-1 at the Vet.

Bonus: Johnson, Moe Elewonibi, Kurt Gouveia, Raleigh McKenzie, Art Monk and Barry Wilburn.

THE TRADING BLOCK

1. Receiver Clifton McNeil, tight end Mack Alston, offensive tackle Jim Snowden, defensive end Mike Fanucci and safety Jeff Severson.

2. Running back Dick James and defensive tackle Andy Stynchula.

3. From the Los Angeles Raiders for quarterback Jay Schroeder.

4. Quarterback Norm Snead and defensive back Claude Crabb. The Eagles also sent linebacker Jimmy Carr to the Redskins.

5. For their top choice in the 1962 draft, running back Ernie Davis. The Heisman Trophy winner from Syracuse would never play a down for the Browns before succumbing to leukemia.

6. Tim Johnson came from Pittsburgh for a fourth-rounder in 1991. Eric Williams came from Detroit for running back James Wilder and another fourth-rounder. The Redskins, who had missed the playoffs the previous two years, went 5-2 in postseason with Johnson and Williams, winning the Super Bowl in 1991.

7. Running back Mike Oliphant.

8. They sent their first-round choice in 1976 to Miami for Theismann, who had already played three years for Toronto of the Canadian Football League.

9. Linebacker Tom Roussel and their fourth and eighth picks in the 1971 draft.

10. From the Rams in exchange for their first-round choice in the 1969 draft. Beban, who had starred at UCLA, had been Los Angeles' second pick in 1968 but hadn't signed. Beban failed at four positions in Washington, barely playing in five games over two years before being cut.

Bonus: Defensive tackle Diron Talbert, linebackers Maxie Baughn, Jack Pardee and Myron Pottios, guard John Wilbur and running back Jeff Jordan. They were acquired for McKeever plus Washington's first and third picks in 1971 and its third, fourth, fifth, sixth and seventh choices in 1972. The Rams also sent their fifth selection in 1971 to the Redskins. Safety Richie Petitbon arrived from Los Angeles in a trade later that year.

PLAYING THE MARKET

1. Running backs John Riggins (Jets) and Calvin Hill (Dallas) and tight end Jean Fugett (Dallas). Hill had played for Hawaii of the World Football League in 1975.

2. Chicago linebacker Wilber Marshall.

3. Running back Herb Mul-Key. He hadn't even gone to college, but Mul-Key went to the 1973 Pro Bowl as the NFC's return specialist.

4. Louisville's Joe Jacoby wasn't much of a defensive lineman, but he was one of the best offensive tackles in NFL history.

5. Center Jeff Bostic, who failed to make the Eagles in 1980, started for Washington from 1981-93.

6. Linebacker Ken Harvey (Phoenix, 1994), punter Reggie Roby (Miami, 1994), halfback Terry Allen (Minnesota, 1995), cornerback Cris Dishman (Houston, 1997).

7. Henry Ellard, who arrived from the Los Angeles Rams in 1994.

8. Linebackers Carl Banks (Giants) and Rick Graf (Houston), receiver Tim McGee (Cincinnati), tight end Jim Riggs (Cincinnati) and defensive end Al Noga (Minnesota). None made the team in 1994.

9. Seven. Center John Gesek (1994), tight end Scott Galbraith (1995), safety James Washington (1995), kicker Eddie Murray (1995), linebacker Darrick Brownlow (1995), linebacker Matt Vanderbeek (1995) and receiver Alvin Harper (1997). Tight end Coleman Bell (1994) had been on the Cowboys' practice squad.

10. Defensive end Charles Mann (San Francisco, 1994) and guard Mark Schlereth (Denver, 1997). Receiver Desmond Howard, the kick-returning MVP of Green Bay's Super Bowl victory in 1996, went to Jacksonville in the 1995 expansion draft.

Bonus: Safeties Brad Edwards and Danny Copeland, cornerback Martin Mayhew, linebacker Matt Millen, defensive end Fred Stokes and tight end Ron Middleton.

HE'S THE BOSS

1. George Allen was 2-0 at home in postseason, winning both in 1972.

2. Lombardi's Redskins went 7-5-2 in 1969 for their first winning season since 1955.

3. Herman Ball was 4-16 (.200) from 1949-51.

4. Dud DeGroot led the Redskins to a 14-5-1 (.725) record in 1944-45.

5. Richie Petitbon was a safety in 1972 and an assistant coach in 1982, 1983, 1987 and 1991. However, Petitbon went just 4-12 in 1993, his lone season as Washington's head coach.

6. Gibbs was 12-12 (1-0 in postseason). Allen was 7-8 (1-0 in postseason).

7. Chicago, 24-7, at Soldier Field.

8. Hall of Famer Ray Flaherty (54-21-3), who won titles in 1937 and 1942.

9. Three. Marv Levy (Kansas City, Buffalo) coached special teams. Ted Marchibroda (Baltimore, Indianapolis) was the offensive coordinator and Mike McCormack (Philadelphia, Baltimore) directed the offensive line. The 1972 Redskins also had three players who would become coaches: linebacker Jack Pardee (Chicago, Washington and Houston), quarterback Sam Wyche (Cincinnati and Tampa Bay) and safety Petitbon (Washington).

10. Bill Austin.

Bonus: None. In contrast, since 1945 the Redskins have made the playoffs 13 times with a Republican in the White House (1971-74, 1976, 1982-84, 1986-87 and 1990-92).

CLASHING WITH THE CARDS

1. Jim Hart in 1984.

2. Two first-round picks and a second-rounder. The Redskins received fifth-, sixth- and 15th-round choices along with Butz.

3. Offensive line coach Jim Hanifan.

4. Offensive backfield coach.

5. Jay Schroeder.

6. Nothing. Fischer had played out his option.

7. Terry Metcalf.

8. Safety Richie Petitbon, who would become Washington's coach 22 years later.

9. Baugh set the club record with six touchdown passes.

10. Eddie Brown, who went to the Pro Bowl that season and in 1977.

Bonus: Washington was 17-10 against Chicago and a slightly worse 32-20-1 against St. Louis. Washington's just 11-9 against Phoenix-Arizona.

1. Terry Allen with 1,353 in 1996.

2. Cliff Battles in 1937.

3. Mike Thomas gained 1,101 yards in 1976.

4. Wilbur Jackson.

5. Frank Akins in 1945.

6. Rob Goode with seven in 1951.

7. Quarterback Joe Theismann (5.1). Choo Choo Justice (4.8) is the top running back.

8. Jamie Morris with 45 against Cincinnati in 1988.

9. Gerald Riggs with 221 against Philadelphia in 1989.

10. Wayne Morris of the St. Louis Cardinals in 1978.

Bonus: Cleveland's Bobby Mitchell rushed for 234 yards against the Redskins in a 1959 game.

PLAYOFF TIME

1. Charley Malone.

2. Cap Boso.

3. Manny Sistrunk.

4. Chicago's Steve Fuller in 1984.

5. Alvin Garrett.

6. Fred Stokes against Minnesota on January 2, 1993.

7. Wade Wilson.

8. Linebacker Kurt Gouveia.

9. Running back Moses Denson and strangely, Mike Bragg. Normally Washington's punter, Bragg was filling in for injured kicker Mark Moseley. Bragg kicked a field goal and added an extra point after Denson's touchdown.

10. Kilmer spent much of the week in the hospital with a stomach disorder.

Bonus: The Raiders.

MANY HAPPY RETURNS

1. Eddie Brown against Tampa Bay in 1977.

2. John Williams averaged 15.3 yards in 1953 and 12.8 yards in 1952-53, the two years he played for the Redskins.

3. Joe Theismann.

4. Rickie Harris from 1965-70.

5. Rickie Harris in 1970.

6. John Williams in 1953, Scooter Scudero in 1958 and Mike Nelms in 1981.

7. With a 69-yard touchdown in the 1991 opener against Detroit, Washington's first punt return score in a decade.

8. Kevin Williams of Dallas in 1994.

9. Eddie Brown in 1977.

10. Dick Todd averaged 17 yards a return in 1941.

Bonus: Andy Farkas (1943), Bert Zagers (1957), Dick James (1963) and Speedy Duncan (1971).

THE BIG PLAYS

1. Billy Wells raced 88 yards for a score against the Chicago Cardinals in 1954.

2. Barry Wilburn went 100 yards against Minnesota in 1987.

3. Ken Jenkins against Pittsburgh in 1985.

4. Bill Dudley went 96 yards for a score against Pittsburgh in 1950.

5. Ollie Matson of the Chicago Cardinals returned a kickoff 105 yards in 1956.

6. Darrell Green ran 78 yards for a score against Indianapolis in 1993.

7. Larry Jones dashed 102 yards against Philadelphia in 1974

8. The Raiders' Jim Plunkett and Cliff Branch in 1983.

9. Cleveland's Bobby Mitchell ran 90 yards in 1959.

10. Minnesota's Charlie West went 98 yards for a score in 1968.

Bonus: Andy Farkas from Frank Filchock vs. Pittsburgh in 1939; Bobby Mitchell from George Izo vs. Cleveland in 1963; Gerry Allen from Sonny Jurgensen against Chicago in 1968.

AT THE TOP

1. Detroit running back Andy Farkas in 1938. The franchise was
   still located in Boston when TCU quarterback Sammy Baugh was
   picked in 1937.

2. Smith, a cornerback from Oregon, was Washington's last first-
   round choice for 13 years mostly due to George Allen's trades.

3. The running back from George Washington, a second-rounder in
   1958, was the Redskins' first top pick not to be taken in the
   first round.

4. TCU tackle Hale (1939) and Penn State offensive tackle Johnson
   (1996) are the Redskins' first and last first-rounders not to
   have played for the team.

5. Texas A&I cornerback Darrell Green in 1983.

6. Idaho fullback Ray McDonald in 1967.

7. Yes. Princeton's Charley Gogolak was Washington's first-rounder in 1966.

8. Maryland running back Ed Vereb in 1956.

9. Jack Scarbath.

10. Tackle Mark May, Washington's top pick in 1981 from Pitt, made the Pro
    Bowl in 1988.

Bonus: UCLA's Cal Rossi in 1946 and 1947. The first selection was
nullified when Rossi was found to have been ineligible for the draft.

THE LATER ROUNDS

1. Central Arkansas linebacker Monte Coleman (1979-94) played during the administrations of Carter, Reagan, Bush and Clinton.

2. Idaho center Mark Schlereth, a 10th-rounder in 1989, played in the Pro Bowl as a guard following the 1991 season.

3. Indiana guard Quinn Buckner.

4. Columbia offensive tackle George Starke (11th round, 1971), Southern Colorado receiver Frank Grant (13th, 1972), Delaware defensive tackle Dennis Johnson (13th, 1973) and UNLV running back Mike Thomas (fifth, 1975).

5. Two-time decathlon gold medalist Bob Mathias as a Stanford back on the 30th round.

6. Kentucky end Howard Schnellenberger on the 21st round. Schnellenberger guided Miami to the title in 1983.

7. North Carolina linebacker Chris Hanburger in 1965.

8. Mississippi quarterback Charlie Conerly on the 11th round. Conerly went on to star for the Giants.

9. It included six future starters: Pitt offensive tackle Mark May (1st); Pitt guard Russ Grimm (3rd); Oklahoma State defensive end Dexter Manley (fifth); South Carolina State receiver Charlie Brown (8th); Rice guard (soon moved to defensive tackle) Darryl Grant (9th) and Portland State receiver (soon moved to tight end) Clint Didier (11th).

10. Texas A&I cornerback Darrell Green (1st round, 1983), Eastern Washington offensive tackle Ed Simmons (6th, 1987) and Southwestern Louisiana running back Brian Mitchell (5th, 1990).

Bonus: The Redskins took Arizona State running back Charley Taylor (later switched to receiver) and Iowa defensive back Paul Krause with their top two picks in 1964.

SAC-K-INGS

1. Defensive end Dexter Manley (1981-89) recorded 97 1/2.

2. Ten vs. Tampa Bay in 1977.

3. Nine in 1991.

4. Linebacker Marvcus Patton.

5. Dallas tackle Ray Childress.

6. Tackle Marc Boutte.

7. Arizona linebacker Jamir Miller.

8. Manley (1988 vs. the Giants) and tackle Diron Talbert (1975 vs. the Giants).

9. Monte Coleman with 56 1/2.

10. Brian Walker.

Bonus: Manley (18 in 1986, 15 in 1985, 13 1/2 in 1984); end Coy Bacon (15 in 1979); end Charles Mann (14 1/2 in 1985); linebacker Ken Harvey (13 1/2 in 1994); end Verlon Biggs (13 in 1973) and tackle Bill Brundidge (13 in 1973).

THE SUPER BOWLS

1. Mike Bass ran 49 yards with a fumble after Miami's Garo Yepremian had his field goal attempt blocked and then tried to pass the ball.

2. Joe Washington.

3. Don McNeal.

4. Alvin Walton.

5. Brad Edwards.

6. Chip Lohmiller (13).

7. Ravin Caldwell.

8. Alvin Garrett.

9. Kim Bokamper.

10. Verlon Biggs (New York Jets, Super Bowl III) and Roy Jefferson (Baltimore Colts, Super Bowl V).

Bonus: Gary Clark and Ricky Sanders each caught 10 passes.

The Final Score

300-352 correct — You're a Hall of Famer

275-300 — Definite Pro Bowler

250-274 — You're a starter

225-249 — You've made the team

Below 225 — You must be a Cowboys fan

JACK KENT COOKE STADIUM   *Photo courtesy of the Washington Redskins*

THE REDSKINS BY THE NUMBERS

0
JOHN OLZEWSKI, RB 1958-60

00
STEVE BAGARUS, RB 1945-46, 48

1
Reggie Roby, P 1993-94
MATT TURK, P 1995-97

2
Jack Weil, P 1987
Ralf Mojsiejenko, P 1989-90
KELLY GOODBURN, P 1990-93
Eddie Murray, K 1995

3
Ralph Guglielmi, QB 1955, 58-60
Charlie Gogolak, K 1966-68
MARK MOSELEY, K 1974-86

4
MIKE BRAGG, P 1968-79
Jess Atkinson, K 1986-87

5
CURT KNIGHT, K 1969-73
Jeff Hayes, P 1982-85
Obed Ariri, K 1987
Heath Shuler, QB 1994-96

6
ALI HAJI-SHEIKH, K 1987

7
JOE THEISMANN, QB 1974-85

8
Bob Holly, QB 1983
CHIP LOHMILLER, K 1988-94

9
SONNY JURGENSEN, QB 1964-74

10
Rudy Bukich, QB 1957-58
Eagle Day, QB 1959-60
Mike Connell, P 1980-81
JAY SCHROEDER, QB 1985-87
Jeff Rutledge, QB 1990-92
Trent Green, QB 1997

11
Ernie Pinckert, RB 1937-40
Cecil Hare, RB 1941-42, 45
Al Fiorentino, G 1943-44
Harvey Jones, DB 1947
Fred Wyant, QB 1956
Jim Ninowski, QB 1967-68
Kim McQuilken, QB 1979
MARK RYPIEN, QB 1988-93

12
Eddie Britt, RB 1937
Boyd Morgan, RB 1939-40
John Goodyear, RB 1942
Lou Rymkus, T 1943
Larry Fuller, RB 1944-45
Herb Shoener, E 1948-49
Harry Gilmer, QB 1948-52, 54
Neil Ferris, DB 1951-52
Randy Johnson, QB 1975
Tom Flick, QB 1980
Steve Cox, P 1985-88
Cary Conklin, QB 1992-93
GUS FREROTTE, QB 1994-97

13

Ed Justice, RB 1937-42
Larry Johnson, C 1944
Ray Monaco, G 1944
Frank Ryan, QB 1969-70
JAKE SCOTT, S 1976-78
Chris Jacke, K 1997

14

Tilly Manton, RB 1938
Al Krueger, E 1941-42
Alex Piasecky, E 1943-45
Tom Miller, E 1945
John Lookabaugh, WR 1946-47
Tom Farmer, RB 1947-48
Billy Cox, RB 1951-52, 55
EDDIE LEBARON, QB 1952-53, 55-59
Dick Shiner, QB 1964-66
Tom Barnhardt, P 1988
Max Zendejas, K 1986

15

JIM BARBER, T 1937-41
George Watts, T 1942
Bob Sneddon, RB 1944
Al Couppee, G 1946
John Hollar, RB 1948-49
Johnny Papit, RB 1951-53
George Izo, QB 1961-64
Mike Kruczek, QB 1980
Tony Robinson, QB 1987
Dave Archer, QB 1988
Greg Coleman, P 1988
Jeff Hostetler, QB 1997

16

Steve Slivinski, G 1939-43
Everett Sharp, T 1944-45
John Steber, G 1946-50
Al Dorow, QB 1954-56
NORM SNEAD, QB 1961-63
Gary Beban, QB 1968-69
Richie Petitbon, S 1971-72
Ed Rubbert, QB 1987
Stan Humphries, QB 1989-90
Rich Gannon, QB 1993

Jeff Query, WR 1995
Scott Blanton, K 1996-97

17

TURK EDWARDS, T 1937-40
Fred Davis, T 1941-42, 45
Mack Reynolds, QB 1960
Galen Hall, QB 1962
Harry Theofiledes, QB 1968
Billy Kilmer, QB 1971-78
Jim Hart, QB 1984
Doug Williams, QB 1986-89
John Friesz, QB 1994

18

Ed Michaels, G 1937
Hank Bartos, G 1938
Bud Erickson, C 1938-39
Bob Titchenal, 1940-42
Ken Hayden, C 1943
Frank Akins, RB 1943-46
Pete Marcus, E 1944
Joe Duckworth, WR 1947
Art Macioszczyk, RB 1948
Ed Berrang, E 1949-52
JACK SCARBATH, QB 1953-54
Sam Wyche, QB 1971-72

19

CHARLEY MALONE, E 1937-40
Joe Aguirre, E-K 1941, 43-45
Jim Peebles, E 1946-49, 51
Eagle Day, QB 1959-60
Dan Pierce, RB 1970

20

CLIFF BATTLES, RB 1937
George Karamatic, RB 1938
Bob Seymour, RB 1940-41, 43-45
Dan Sandifer, DB 1948-49
George Thomas, RB 1950-51
Jules Rykovich, RB 1952-53
George Rosso, DB 1953
Hal Norris, DB 1955-56
Doyle Nix, RB 1958-59
Ed Vereb, RB 1960
Bob Freeman, RB 1962
Frank Budd, WR 1963
Fred Mazurek, RB 1965-66
Gerry Allen, RB 1967-69
Tommy Mason, RB 1971
Ken Stone, S 1973-75
Joe Lavender, CB 1976-82
Michael Morton, RB 1985
Lionel Vital, RB 1987
Herb Welch, S 1989
Alvoid Mays, CB 1990-94
Marc Logan, RB 1995-97

21

Swede Olsson, G 1937-38
Dick Farman, G 1939-43
Frank Walton, G 1944-45
Bill Ward, C 1946-47
Don Deeks, T 1947
Rob Goode, RB 1949-51, 54-55
Roy Barni, DB 1955-56
Gary Glick, DB 1959-60
Doyle Schick, LB 1961
Jim Carr, LB 1964-65
Gene Mingo, K 1967
George Harold, DB 1968
Tom Brown, DB 1969
Larry Jones, KR 1974-77
MIKE NELMS, KR 1980-84
Tim Jessie, RB 1987
Earnest Byner, RB 1989-93
Deral Boykin, CB 1994
Terry Allen, RB 1995-97

22

Chuck Bond, T 1937-38
Roy Zimmerman, QB 1940-42
Doug Turley, DE 1944-48
Harry Dowda, DB 1949-53
Choo Choo Justice, RB 1950, 1952-54
Jim Crotty, DB 1960-61
Leroy Jackson, RB 1962-63
Dan Lewis, RB 1965
T.J. Jackson, WR 1967
Jim Harris, DB 1970
Roosevelt Taylor, S 1972
MIKE THOMAS, RB 1975-78
Buddy Hardeman, RB 1979-80
Curtis Jordan, S 1981-86
Danny Burmeister, DB 1987
Jamie Morris, RB 1988-89
Todd Bowles, S 1986-90, 92-93
Johnny Thomas, CB 1988, 90, 92-94
Frank Wycheck, TE 1993-94
Eric Sutton, CB 1996

23

Don Irwin, RB 1937-39
Keith Birlem, DB 1939
Elmer Madarik, DB 1948
Hall Haynes, DB 1950, 53
Claude Crabb, CB 1962-63
Bill Hunter, WR 1965
BRIG OWENS, S 1966-77
Tony Peters, S 1979-82, 84-85
Todd Bowles, S 1986-90, 92-93
Sebastian Savage, CB 1995
Robert Bailey, CB 1995
Tomur Barnes, CB 1997

24

Jay Turner, LB 1938-39
Howie Livingston, DB 1948-50
Leon Heath, RB 1951-53
Blackie Kincaid, DB 1954
Jim Podoley, RB 1957-60
Johnny Sample, CB 1963-65
Ron Rector, RB 1966
Pete Larson, RB 1967-68
Bob Wade, DB 1969
BILL MALINCHAK, WR 1970-74, 76
Spencer Thomas, S 1975
Lemar Parrish, CB 1978-81
Joe Washington, RB 1981-84
Anthony Washington, CB 1983-84
Kelvin Bryant, RB 1986-88, 90
Carl Harry, WR 1989, 92
Pat Eilers, S 1993-94
Stanley Richard, S 1995-97

25

Max Krause, RB 1937-40
Ken Dow, RB 1941
Dick Poillon, K 1942, 46-49
Frank Seno, RB 1943-44, 49
John Doolan, DB 1945
Hardy Brown, LB 1950
John Papit, RB 1951-53
Nick Aducci, LB 1954-55
Tom Runnels, RB 1956-57
Dick Lynch, DB 1958
Richie McCabe, DB 1959
Joe Krakoski, DB 1961
Pervis Atkins, RB 1964-65
A.D. Whitfield, RB 1966-68
Mike Hull, RB 1971-74
Eddie Brown, S 1975-77
Benny Malone, RB 1978-79
Curtis Jordan S, 1981-86
JOE WASHINGTON, RB 1981-84
Dave Etherly, DB 1987
Mike Oliphant, RB 1988
Reggie Dupard, RB 1989-90
Mickey Washington, CB 1992
Pat Eilers, S 1992
Tom Carter, CB 1993-96

26

Vic Carroll, T 1937-42
Vernon Foltz, C 1944
Al Lolotai, G 1945
Ralph Ruthstrom, LB 1947
Jim Castiglia, RB 1947-48
Tom Cochran, RB 1949
Frank Spaniel, RB 1950
Ed Salem, QB 1951
Andy Davis, DB 1953
Don Shula, DB 1957
Bill Stits, DB 1959
PAUL KRAUSE, S 1964-67
Bob Brunet, RB 1969, 70-77
Don Harris, S 1978-79
Terry Metcalf, RB 1981
Reggie Evans, RB 1983
Ricky Smith, CB 1984
Rick Badjanek, RB 1986
Wayne Wilson, RB 1987
Craig McEwen, TE 1987-88
Wayne Davis, CB 1989-90
Danny Copeland, S 1991-93
Alan Grant, CB 1994
Muhammad Oliver, CB 1995
Cris Dishman, CB 1997

27

Mickey Parks, C 1938-40
Jim Stuart, OT 1941
Joe Zeno, G 1942-44
Earl Audet, T 1945
Joe Bartos, RB 1950
Neil Ferris, DB 1951-52
Don Menasco, DB 1954
Art DeCarlo, DB 1956-57
Mike Sommer, RB 1958-59, 61
John Love, WR 1967
KEN HOUSTON, S 1973-80
Brad Edwards, S 1990-93
Keith Taylor S 1994-96

28

Nels Peterson, WR 1937
Bob Masterson, E 1938-43
Ralph Schilling, DE 1946
Bones Taylor, WR 1947-54
Scooter Scudero, DB 1954-58
Ted Rzempoluch, DB 1963
Ozzie Clay, WR 1964
Dick Smith, DB 1967-68
Jon Henderson, WR 1979
Alvin Haymond, KR 1972
Herb Mul-Key, RB 1972-74
Trent Bryant, CB 1981
Cris Crissy, WR 1981
DARRELL GREEN, CB 1983-97

29

Jim Karcher, G 1937-39
Steve Andrako, C 1940-41
Bill DeCorrevont, DB 1945
Oscar Britt, G 1946
George Wilde, RB 1947
Howard Hartley, DB 1948
Jack Dwyer, DB 1951
Paul Barry, RB 1953
Bert Zagers, DB 1955, 57-58
Ted Vactor, CB 1969-73
MARK MURPHY, S 1977-84
Reggie Branch, RB 1985-89
David Gulledge, S 1992
Keith Taylor, S 1994
Scott Turner, CB 1995-97

30

Dixie Howell, RB 1937
Frank Filchock, QB 1938-41, 44-45
Steve Juzwik, RB 1942
Coye Dunn, RB 1943
Jim Youel, QB 1946-48
Ed Sutton, RB 1957-59
Jim Cunningham, RB 1961-63
Bob Briggs, RB 1965
Jeff Jordan, RB 1971-72
Bryant Salter, DB 1974-75
Jim Kiick, RB 1977
Ike Forte, RB 1978-80
Nick Giaquinto, RB 1981-83
Jeff Moore, RB 1984

Reggie Branch, RB 1985-89
Dwight Garner, RB 1986
Walter Holman, RB 1987
Joe Mickles, RB 1989
BRIAN MITCHELL, RB 1990-97

31

Jimmy Johnston, DB 1939-40
Frank Clair, E 1941
Larry Weldon, QB 1944-45
Clyde Ehrhardt, C 1946, 48-49
DON BOSSELER, RB 1957-64
Joe Kantor, RB 1966
Charley Harraway, RB 1969-73
Charlie Evans, RB 1974
Ken Jenkins, RB 1985-86
Clarence Vaughn, S 1987-91
Gregory Clifton, WR 1993
Darryl Pounds, DB 1995-97

32

Bob McChesney, E 1937-42
George Cafego, QB 1943
Sal Rosato, RB 1945-47
Pete Stout, RB 1949-50
Leon Heath, RB 1951-53
Leo Elter, RB 1955-57
Jim Wulff, DB 1960-61
Billy Ray Barnes, RB 1962-63
Billy Clay, DB 1966
Ray McDonald, RB 1967-68
Henry Dyer, RB 1969-70
JACK PARDEE, LB 1971-72
Mike Curtis, LB 1977-78
Vernon Dean, CB 1982-87
Craig McEwen, TE 1987-88
James Wilder, RB 1990
Ricky Ervins, RB 1991-94
Keith Thibodeaux, CB 1997

33

SAMMY BAUGH, QB 1937-52

34

Bill Hartman, RB 1938
Jimmy German, QB 1939
Sandy Sanford, E 1940
Mike Micka, DB 1944-45
Jim Gaffney, RB 1946
Ed Quirk, RB 1948-50
John Cloud, RB 1952-53
Yazoo Smith, CB 1968
TONY GREEN, KR 1978
Bobby Hammond, RB 1979-80
Kevin Williams, CB 1985, 88
Brian Davis, CB 1987-90
Garry Kimble, DB 1987
Terry Hoage, S 1991
Martin Bayless, S 1994

35

Riley Smith, QB 1937-38
WILBUR MOORE, RB 1939-46
Bill Dudley, RB 1950-51, 53
Joe Don Looney, RB 1966-67
Calvin Hill, RB 1976-77
Jack Deloplaine, RB 1978
Lonnie Perrin, RB 1979
Rickey Claitt, RB 1980-81
Keith Griffin, RB 1984-88
Martin Mayhew, CB 1989-92
Leomont Evans, S 1996-97

36

Wee Willie Wilkin, T 1938-43
Hank Harris, G 1947-48
CHUCK DRAZENOVICH, LB 1950-59
Ron Hatcher, RB 1962
Tom Tracy, RB 1963-64
Tom Barrington, RB 1966
Ralph Nelson, RB 1975
Eddie Moss, RB 1977
Timmy Smith, RB 1987-88
Joe Cofer, DB 1987
Frank Wycheck, TE 1993-94
William Bell, RB 1994-96

37

Bill Young, T 1937-42, 46
Joe Pasqua, T 1943

Jim Watson, C 1945
Joe Tereshinski, DE 1947-54
J.W. Lockett, RB 1964
PAT FISCHER, CB 1968-77
Raphel Cherry, S 1985
Kevin Williams, CB 1985-88
Charles Jackson, S 1987
Travis Curtis, S 1988, 91
Gerald Riggs, RB 1989-91
Darryl Morrison, S 1993-96
Cedric Smith, FB 1994-95
James Washington, S 1995
Jesse Campbell, S 1997

38

Ben Smith, E 1937
Hal Bradley, E 1938-39
Bob Fisher, T 1940
Jack Jenkins, RB 1943, 46-47
Bill Conkright, C 1943
Les Dye, E 1944-45
Clyde Goodnight, WR 1949-50
Jim Martin, K 1964
John Seedborg, P 1965
Rick Casares, RB 1965
Larry Willis, S 1973
Larry Smith, RB 1974
Clarence Harmon, RB 1977-82
GEORGE ROGERS, RB 1985-87
Willard Reaves, RB 1989
Darryl Morrison, S 1993-96
David Frisch, TE 1997

39

Ed Kawal, C 1937
Clem Stralka, G 1938-42, 45-46
Zip Hanna, G 1945
George Buksar, LB 1951-52
Bob Sykes, RB 1952
ROB GOODE, RB 1949-51, 54-55
Dave Francis, RB 1963
George Hughley, RB 1965
Otis Wonsley, RB 1981-85
Skip Lane, S 1987
Robert Green, RB 1992
Tyrone Rush, RB 1994

40

WAYNE MILLNER, WR 1937-41, 45
John Kovatch, DE 1942, 46
Frank Ribar, G 1943
Billy Cox, DB 1951-52, 55
Gary Lowe, DB 1956-57
Sam Horner, RB 1960-61
Lonnie Sanders, DB 1963-67
Aaron Martin, DB 1968
Dave Kopay, RB 1969-70
George Nock, RB 1972
Fred Hyatt, WR 1973
Doug Cunningham, RB 1975
Bob Anderson, RB 1975
Windlan Hall, S 1977
Wilbur Jackson, RB 1980-82
Jimmy Smith, RB 1984
Rick Kane, RB 1984
Alvin Walton, S 1986-91
Reggie Brooks, RB 1993-95

41

Red Krause, C 1938
Dick Todd, RB 1939-42, 45-48
Leo Stasica, DB 1943
Billy Wells, RB 1954, 56-57
Sid Watson, RB 1958
Bob Hudson, LB 1959
Jim Steffen, DB 1961-65
MIKE BASS, CB 1969-75
Brian Carpenter, CB 1983-84
Tim Morrison, CB 1986-87
Dennis Woodberry, DB 1987-88
Johnny Thomas, CB 1988, 90, 92-94
Chris Mandeville, DB 1989

42

Dick Tuckey, RB 1938
Ray Hare, RB 1940-43
Jim North, T 1944
John Adams, T 1945-49
Nick Sebek, QB 1950
Dick Alban, DB 1952-55
Jerry Planutis, RB 1956
Bill Anderson, WR 1958-63
CHARLEY TAYLOR, WR 1964-77

43

Eddie Kahn, G 1937
Rink Bond, RB 1938
Ed Cifers, E 1941-42, 46
Nick Campofreda, C 1944
Ernie Barber, C 1945
Len Szafaryn, T 1949
John Williams, DB 1952-53
Vic Janowicz, RB 1954-55
Dick Haley, DB 1959-60
Jim Kerr, DB 1961-62
Tom Walters, DB 1964-67
LARRY BROWN, RB 1969-76

44

Andy Farkas, RB 1938-44
Vito Ananis, RB 1945
Merl Condit, RB 1945
Mike Garzoni, RB 1947
Mike Roussos, T 1948-49
Harry Dowda, DB 1949-53
Nick Adduci, LB 1954-55
Steve Thurlow, RB 1966-68
Jeff Severson, DB 1972
Moses Denson, RB 1974-75
JOHN RIGGINS, RB 1976-79, 81-85

45

Bo Russell, T 1939-40
Bob Hoffman, LB 1940-41
Ed Beinor, T 1941-42
Ted Lapka, E 1943-44, 46
Paul McKee, E 1947-48
Dick Stovall, LB 1949
SAM BAKER, K-P 1953, 56-59
Ralph Felton, LB 1954-60
Speedy Duncan, KR 1971-74
Gerard Williams, CB 1976-78
Jeris White, CB 1980-82
Barry Wilburn, CB 1985-89
Sidney Johnson, CB 1990-92
Brian Walker, S 1996-97

46

Roy Young, T 1938
John Spirida, RB 1939
Jack Banta, RB 1941
Lee Gentry, RB 1941
Joe Gibson, LB 1943
Andy Natowich, RB 1944
Tom Bedore, C 1944
Joe Ungerer, T 1944-45
Paul Stenn, T 1946
Jack Sommer, C 1947
Don Doll, DB 1953
Dale Atkeson, RB 1954-56
Dale Hackbart, DB 1961-63
RICKIE HARRIS, DB 1965-70
Frank Grant, WR 1973-78
LeCharls McDaniel, CB 1981-82
Ricky Sanders, WR 1986-93
Mike Mitchell, CB 1987
Dennis Woodberry, CB 1987-88

47

George Smith, C 1937, 41-43
Jack Keenan, T 1944-45
Ernie Williamson, T 1947
Carl Butkus, OT 1947
Laurie Niemi, T 1949-53
DICK JAMES, RB 1956-63
Jim Shorter, DB 1964-67
Walter Roberts, WR 1969-70
Duane Thomas, RB 1973-74
Ray Waddy, CB 1979-80
Greg Williams, DB 1982-85
Johnny Thomas, CB 1988,90, 92-94
A.J. Johnson, CB 1989-94
Larry Bowie, RB 1996-97

48

Marvin Whited, LB 1942, 45
Tony Leon, G 1943
Lee Presley, C 1945
Weldon Edwards, T 1948
Bob Hendren, T 1949-51
Norb Hecker, DB 1955-57
Ben Scotti, DB 1959-61
Doug Elmore, DB 1962
Angelo Coia, WR 1964-65
John Burrell, WR 1966-67

Jon Jaqua, S 1970-72
KEN COFFEY, S 1983-84, 86
Steve Gage, S 1987-88
Travis Curtis, S 1988, 91
Ken Whisenhunt, TE 1990
Stephen Davis, RB 1996-97

49

Jim Meade, DB 1939-40
John Koniszewski, T 1945-46, 48
John Sanchez, T 1947-49
Sam Venuto, RB 1952
Sam Baker, K-P 1953, 56-59
Jim Monachino, RB 1955
Billy Brewer, DB 1960
BOBBY MITCHELL, WR 1962-68

50

Bob Nussbaumer, DB 1947-48
HARRY ULINSKI, C 1950-51, 53-56
Fred Hageman, LB 1961-64
Willie Adams, DE 1965-66
Maxie Baughn, LB 1974
Pete Wysocki, LB 1975-80
Larry Kubin, LB 1982-84
Ravin Caldwell, LB 1987-92
Jon Kimmel, LB 1987
Carlton Rose, LB 1987
Tom Myslinski, G 1992
Marc Raab, C 1993
Darrick Brownlow, LB 1995-96
Derek Smith, LB 1997

51

Clyde Shugart, G 1939-44
Ed Merkle, G 1944
Reid Lennan, G 1945
Fred Boensch, G 1947-48
Tony Momsen, C 1952
Jim Schrader, C 1954, 56-61
Gordon Kelley, LB 1962-63
John Reger, LB 1964-66
Sid Williams, LB 1967
John Didion, C 1969-70
Bob Grant, LB 1971
Dan Ryczek, C 1973-75
Joe Harris, LB 1977
MONTE COLEMAN, LB 1979-94

52

Harry Gilmer, QB 1948-52, 54
John Allen, C 1955-58
Harry Butsko, LB 1963
Mike Morgan, LB 1968
Gene Hamlin, C 1970
John Pergine, LB 1973-75
NEAL OLKEWICZ, LB 1979-89
Matt Elliott, C 1992
Cory Raymer, C 1995-97

53

Rufus Deal, RB 1942
Jack Smith, DE 1943
Mitch Ucovich, T 1944
Al DeMao, C 1945-53
Torgy Torgeson, LB 1955-57
Bill Roehnelt, LB 1960
Bob Pellegrini, LB 1962-65
Steve Jackson, LB 1966-67
Harold McLinton, LB 1969-78
JEFF BOSTIC, C 1980-93
Marvcus Patton, LB 1995-97

54

Don Corbitt, C 1948
Walt Cudzik, C 1954
Bill Fulcher, LB 1956-58
Don Croftcheck, G 1965-66
Tom Roussel, LB 1968-70
Bob Kuziel, C 1975-80
Kevin Turner, LB 1981
Pete Cronan, LB 1981-85
Joe Krakoski, LB 1986
KURT GOUVEIA, LB 1987-94
John Cowne, C 1987
Al Catanho, LB 1996
Greg Jones, LB 1997

55

Ki Aldrich, C 1941-42, 45-47
Harold Crisler, E 1948-49
Jim Ricca, T 1951-54
Allen Miller, LB 1962-63
CHRIS HANBURGER, LB 1965-78
Mel Kaufman, LB 1981-88
Andre Collins, LB 1990-94

Jeff Uhlenhake, C 1996-97

56

Don Avery, T 1946-47
Harry Ulinski, 1950-51, 53-56
Dick Woodard, C 1952
Charley Brueckman, LB 1958
Frank Kuchta, C 1959
Ed Beatty, C 1961
LEN HAUSS, C 1964-77
Dan Peiffer, C 1980
Quentin Lowry, LB 1981-83
Trey Junkin, LB 1984
Calvin Daniels, LB 1986
Eric Coyle, C 1987
Brian Bonner, LB 1989
Tom Myslinski, G 1992
Rick Hamilton, LB 1993-94
Erick Anderson, LB 1994
Dion Foxx, LB 1995

57

Ed Stacco, T 1948
John Badaczewski, G 1949-51
Dave Crossan, C 1965-69
Stu O'Dell, LB 1974-77
Rich Milot, LB 1979-87
Anthony Copeland, LB 1987
Don Graham, LB 1989
Randy Kirk, LB 1990
Matt Millen, LB 1991
Guy Bingham, C 1992-93
KEN HARVEY, LB 1994-97

58

Leo Nobile, C 1947
Mike Katrishen, G 1948-49
George Burman, C 1971-72
Mike Varty, LB 1973
Don Hover, LB 1978-79
Charlie Weaver, LB 1981
Stuart Anderson, LB 1982-85
Shawn Burks, LB 1986
David Jones, C 1987
David Windham, LB 1987
WILBER MARSHALL, LB 1988-92
Carl Banks, LB 1993
Patrise Alexander, LB 1996-97

59

Jim Carroll, LB 1966-68
BRAD DUSEK, LB 1974-81
Jim Youngblood, LB 1984
Chris Keating, LB 1985
Angelo Snipes, LB 1986
Jeff Paine, LB 1986
Ray Hitchcock, C 1987
Eric Wilson, LB 1987
Mike Scully, C 1988
Dave Harbour, C 1988-89
John Brantley, LB 1992
Chris Sedoris, C 1996

60

John Jaffurs, G 1946
Bill Gray, G 1947-48
Joe Soboleski, G 1949
Buddy Brown, G 1951-52
Marv Berschet, G 1954-55
DICK STANFEL, G 1956-58
Bob Khayat, K 1960, 62-63
Jim Carroll, LB 1966-68
John Wilbur, G 1971-74
Donnie Hickman, G 1978
Gary Anderson, G 1980
Roy Simmons, G 1983
J.T. Turner, G 1984
Dan McQuaid, OT 1985-87
Mike Wootten, C 1987
Fred Stokes, DE 1989-92
Greg Huntington, G 1993

61

Bob DeFruiter, DB 1945-47
Gene Pepper, G 1950-53
FRAN O'BRIEN, OT 1960-66
Jim Avery, TE 1966
Don Bandy, G 1967-68
Dennis Johnson, DT 1974-77
Melvin Jones, G 1981
Ken Huff, G 1983-85
Rick Kehr, G 1987-88
Willard Scissum, G 1987
Mark Adickes, G 1990-91
Vernice Smith, C 1993-95

62

Slug Witucki, 1950-51, 53-56
Don Boll, OT 1953-59
John Nisby, G 1962-64
Darrell Dess, G 1965-66
RAY SCHOENKE, G 1966-75
Dan Nugent, G 1976-78, 80
Don Laster, OT 1982
Mo Towns, OT 1984
Phil Pettey, G 1987
Ralph Tamm, G 1991
Darryl Moore, G 1993

63

Herb Siegert, G 1949-51
Slug Witucki, G 1950-51, 53-56
Emil Karas, LB 1959
Rod Breedlove, LB 1960-64
Mitch Johnson, OT 1966-68
Ed Breding, LB 1967-68
Steve Duich, G 1969
Bruce Kimball, G 1983-84
RALEIGH MCKENZIE, C 1985-94
John Gesek, C 1994-95

64

Ron Marciniak, G 1955
Mitch Johnson, OT 1966-68
MANNY SISTRUNK, DT 1970-75
Ron Saul, G 1976-81
Steve Hamilton, DE 1985-88
Ralph Tamm, G 1991
Moe Elewonibi, OT 1992-93
Trevor Matich, C 1994-96

65

Jim Clark, G 1952-53
Walt Houston, G 1955
Vince Promuto, G 1960-70
Fred Sturt, G 1974
DAVE BUTZ, DT 1975-88

66

Jim Norman, DT 1955
Ed Voytek, G 1957-58
Bob Whitlow, C 1960-61
Carl Kammerer, DE 1963-69
Myron Pottios, LB 1971-73
Martin Imhof, DE 1974
Jim Arneson, G 1975
Ted Fritsch, C 1976-79
JOE JACOBY, OT 1981-93
Dan Turk, C 1997

67

Dave Suminski, G 1953
Red Stephens, G 1955-60
Bernie Darre, G 1961
Andy Cvercko, G 1963
Bob Reed, G 1965
Jake Kupp, G-TE 1966
John Wootten, G 1968
Dan Grimm, G 1969
RUSTY TILLMAN, LB 1970-77
Greg Dubinetz, G 1979
Bruce Kimball, G 1983-84
Tom Beasley, DT 1985
Steve Thompson, DE 1987
Kit Lathrop, DE 1987
Henry Waechter, DE 1987
Ray Brown, G 1989-90, 92-95
Shar Pourdanesh, OT 1996-97

68

Ed Bagdon, G 1952
Knox Ramsey, G 1952-53
Dave Sparks, G 1954
Wiley Feagin, G 1963
Willie Banks, G 1968-69
Mike Fanucci, DE 1972
Jim Harlan, OT 1978
RUSS GRIMM, G 1981-91
Joe Patton, OT 1994-97

69

Ron Hansen, G 1954
Tom Goosby, G 1966
Willie Banks, G 1968-69

Perry Brooks, DT 1978-84
R.C. Thielemann, G 1985-88
MARK SCHLERETH, G 1989-94

70

Lou Karras, DT 1950-52
Dick Modzelewski, DT 1953-54
Fred Miller, OT 1955
Tony Sardisco, G 1956
Ray Lemek, OT 1957-61
Chuck Moore, G 1962
SAM HUFF, LB 1964-67, 69
Will Wynn, DE 1977
Leonard Marshall, DE 1994

71

Jerry Houghton, LB 1950
Will Renfro, DT 1957-59
Andy Stynchula, DE 1960-63
George Seals, DT 1964
Spain Musgrove, DT 1967-69
Frank Bosch, DT 1968-70
Jim Tyrer, OT 1974
Karl Lorch, DE 1976-81
Garry Puetz, OT 1982
CHARLES MANN, DE 1983-93
Ron Lewis, G 1995

72

Jim Staton, DT 1951
Joe Moss, OT 1952
Erik Christensen, DE 1956
Don Owens, DT 1957
Jim Weatherall, DT 1958
Don Churchwell, OT 1959
Joe Rutgens, DT 1961-69
Terry Hermeling, OT 1970-73, 75-80
Diron Talbert, DT 1971-80
DEXTER MANLEY, DE 1981-89
Mike Haight, OT 1992
Al Noga, DE 1993
Romeo Bandison, DT 1995-96
Mike Flores, DE 1995

73

Ken Barfield, T 1954
Mike Davlin, T 1955
John Miller, T 1956, 58-59
Riley Mattson, T 1961-64
Stan Jones, T 1965
Frank Bosch, DE 1968-70
Paul Laaveg, G 1970-75
Jeff Williams, T 1978-80
MARK MAY, G 1981-89
Lamar Mills, DT 1994
Mike Flores, DE 1995
Darryl Ashmore, OT 1996-97

74

Laurie Niemi, OT 1949-53
* Bob Morgan, DT 1954
Ed Khayat, DT 1957, 62-63
Jim Snowden, OT 1965-71
GEORGE STARKE, OT 1973-84
Markus Koch, DE 1986-91
Curtis McGriff, DE 1987
Gerald Nichols, DT 1993
Brian Thure, OT 1995
Brad Badger, G 1997

75

Enrique Ecker, OT 1952
Don Campora, DT 1953
Harry Jagielski, DT 1956
Ben Davidson, DT 1962-63
Fred Williams, DT 1964-65
Rich Marshall, DT 1966
John Kelly, OT 1966-67
Fred Washington, OT 1968
Steve Wright, OT 1970
TERRY HERMELING, OT 1970-73, 75-80
Deacon Jones, DE 1974
Mike Clark, DE 1981
Pat Ogrin, DT 1981-82
Darrick Brilz, G 1987
Mike Stensrud, DT 1989
Eric Williams, DT 1990-93
John Gesek, C 1994-95
Bob Dahl, G 1996-97

76

Paul Lipscomb, T 1950-54
J.D. Kimmel, DT 1955-56
Don Stallings, DE 1960
Jim Prestel, DT 1967
Walt Rock, OT 1968-73
Tim Stokes, OT 1975-77
Bob Heinz, DT 1978
Jerry Scanlan, OT 1980-81
Mat Mendenhall, DE 1981-82
Rick Donnalley, C 1984-85
Ron Tilton, G 1986
ED SIMMONS, OT 1987-97
Frank Frazier, G 1987

77

Jack Jacobs, QB 1946
Tommy Mont, QB 1947-49
Ray Krouse, DT 1960
Steve Barnett, OT 1964
Fred Williams, DT 1964-65
Walter Barnes, DT 1966-68
Bill Brundige, DT 1970-77
Joe Jones, DE 1979-80
DARRYL GRANT, DT 1981-90
Jim Wahler, DT 1992-93
Tre Johnson, G 1994-97

78

Don Lawrence, DT 1959-61
Ron Snidow, DE 1963-67
Floyd Peters, DT 1970
Mike Taylor, OT 1971
Walt Sweeney, G 1974-75
Dallas Hickman, DE 1976-81
Paul Smith, DE 1979-80
Tony McGee, DE 1982-84
Dean Hamel, DT 1985-88
Lybrant Robinson, DE 1989
TIM JOHNSON, DT 1990-95
Ryan Kuehl, DT 1996-97
Chris Zorich, DT 1997

79

John Yonakor, DE 1952
Bill Hegarty, OT 1953
Volney Peters, DT 1954-57
Bob Toneff, DT 1959-64
Dennis Crane, DT 1968-69
Ron McDole, DE 1971-78
Coy Bacon, DE 1978-81
Pat Ogrin, DT 1981-82
Todd Liebenstein, DE 1982-85
Doug Barnett, DE 1985
Mark Carlson, OT 1987
JIM LACHEY, OT 1988-92, 94-95
Steve Emtman, DT 1997

80

Enrique Ecker, OT 1952
GENE BRITO, DE 1951-53, 55-58
Steve Junker, WR 1961-62
Joe Hernandez, WR 1964
Pat Hodgson, WR 1966
Bruce Alford, K 1967
Bob Long, WR 1969
Roy Jefferson, WR 1971-76
Coy Bacon, DE 1978-81
John McDaniel, WR 1978-80
Kris Haines, WR 1979
Virgil Seay, WR 1981-84
Malcolm Barnwell, WR 1985
Joe Phillips, WR 1985, 87
Eric Yarber, WR 1986-87
Teddy Wilson, WR 1987
Derrick Shepard, WR 1987-88
Joe Johnson, WR 1989-91
Desmond Howard, WR 1992-94
Olanda Truitt, WR 1994-95
Bill Brooks, WR 1996

81

Dan Brown, DE 1950
Sam Morley, WR 1954
Joe Walton, WR 1957-60
Lew Luce, RB 1961
Bob Jencks, K 1965
Jake Kupp, TE-G 1966
Ken Barefoot, TE 1968
Leo Carroll, DE 1969-70

Mack Alston, TE 1970-72
Doug Winslow, WR 1976
Terry Anderson, WR 1978
J.T. Smith, WR 1978
Chris DeFrance, WR 1979
ART MONK, WR 1980-93

82

Ed Berrang, DE 1949-52
Roland Dale, DE 1950
Fran Polsfoot, WR 1953
JOHN CARSON, WR 1954-59
Ken MacAfee, WR 1959
Pat Heenan, WR 1960
Dick Absher, K 1967
Clark Miller, DE 1969
Jimmie Jones, DE 1971-73
Dallas Hickman, DE 1976-81
Rich Caster, TE 1981-82
John Sawyer, TE 1983
Anthony Jones, TE 1984-88
Joe Caravello, TE 1987-88
John Brandes, TE 1990-92
Ray Rowe, TE 1992-93
Jim Riggs, TE 1993
Kurt Haws, TE 1994
Michael Westbrook, WR 1995-97

83

Paul Dekker, WR 1953
Charlie Jones, E 1955
Ed Meadows, DE 1959
Roy Wilkins, LB 1960-61
Jim Norton, DT 1969
Bruce Anderson, DE 1970
Ricky Thompson, WR 1978-81
Mark McGrath, WR 1983-85
Dave Stief, WR 1983
Rich Mauti, WR 1984
James Noble, WR 1986
RICKY SANDERS, WR 1986-93
Richard Johnson, WR 1987
Craig McEwen, TE 1987-88
Tydus Winans, WR 1994-95
Flipper Anderson, WR 1996
Albert Connell, WR 1997

84

Bones Taylor, WR 1947-54
Herb Shoener, DE 1948-49
Tom Braatz, LB 1957-59
Tom Osborne, WR 1960-61
Mike Hancock, TE 1973-74
Jean Fugett, TE 1976-79
Greg McCrary, TE 1978, 81
Zion McKinney, WR 1980
Mike Williams, TE 1982-84
Walt Arnold, TE 1984
Rich Mauti, WR 1984
GARY CLARK, WR 1985-92
Joe Phillips, WR 1987
Keiron Bigby, WR 1987
Mark Stock, WR 1993
Olanda Truitt, WR 1994-95
Jamie Asher, TE 1995-97

85

Walt Yowarsky, E 1951, 54
John Paluck, DE 1956, 59-65
Tom Braatz, LB 1957-59
Gene Cronin, DE 1961-62
Bill Quinlan, DE 1965
Marlin McKeever, LB 1968-70
John Hoffman, DE 1969-70
Clifton McNeil, WR 1971-72
Willie Holman, DE 1973
Brian Fryer, WR 1976
Greg McCrary, TE 1978, 81
DON WARREN, TE 1979-92
Dave Truitt, TE 1987
Tim McGee, WR 1993
Henry Ellard, WR 1994-97

86

Steve Meilinger, WR 1956-57
JOHN PALUCK, DE 1956, 59-65
Bill Briggs, DE 1966-67
Marlin McKeever, LB 1968-70
Verlon Biggs, DE 1971-74
Boyd Dowler, WR 1971
Bill Larson, TE 1977
John McDaniel, WR 1978-80
Phil DuBois, TE 1979-80
Bob Raba, TE 1981

Clint Didier, TE 1982-87
Marvin Williams, TE 1987
Mike Tice, TE 1989
Stephen Hobbs, WR 1990-92
Leslie Shepherd, WR 1994-97

87

Clyde Goodnight, WR 1949-50
Ed Barker, WR 1954
Ralph Thomas, WR 1955-56
Ed Khayat, DT 1957, 62-63
Fred Dugan, WR 1961-63
JERRY SMITH, TE 1965-77
Charlie Brown, WR 1982-84
Terry Orr, TE 1986-90, 92-93
K.D. Dunn, TE 1987
Ron Middleton, TE 1988, 90-93
Coleman Bell, TE 1995
James Thrash, WR 1997

88

Jerry Hennessey, DE 1952-53
Chet Ostrowski, DE 1954-59
Dick Lasse, LB 1960-61
PAT RICHTER, TE 1963-70
Alvin Reed, TE 1973-75
Danny Buggs, WR 1976-79
Doc Walker, TE 1980-85
Derek Holloway, WR 1986
Todd Frain, TE 1986
Cliff Benson, TE 1987
Derrick Shepard, WR 1987-88
Craig McEwen, TE 1987-88
Joe Caravello, TE 1987-88
White Shoes Johnson, KR 1988
Ron Middleton, TE 1988, 90-93
Jimmie Johnson, TE 1989-91
James Jenkins, TE 1991-97

89

JOE TERESHINSKI, DE 1947-54
Bob Dee, DE 1957-58
Art Gob, DE 1959-60
John Aveni, K 1961
Hugh Smith, WR 1962
Jim Collier, TE 1963
Preston Carpenter, WR 1964-66
Leo Carroll, DE 1969-70
Verlon Biggs, DE 1971-74
Dave Robinson, LB 1973-74
Reggie Haynes, TE 1978
Grady Richardson, WR 1979-80
Kenny Harrison, WR 1980
Alvin Garrett, WR 1981-84
Calvin Muhammad, WR 1984-85
Clarence Verdin, WR 1986-87
Terry Orr, TE 1986-90, 92-93
Glenn Dennison, TE 1987
Anthony Allen, WR 1987-88
Walter Stanley, WR 1990
Ethan Horton, TE 1994
Scott Galbraith, TE 1995-96
Chris Thomas, WR 1997

90

Walt Arnold, TE 1984
Bobby Curtis, LB 1987
Huey Richardson, LB 1992
Rick Graf, LB 1993
Tyronne Stowe, LB 1994
Terry Crews, LB 1995
Troy Barnett, DT 1996
KENARD LANG, DE 1997

91

Tony Settles, LB 1987
GREG MANUSKY, LB 1988-90
Shane Collins, DE 1992-94
Matt Vanderbeek, LB 1995-96
Chris Mims, DT 1997

92

Derek Bunch, LB 1987
DEXTER NOTTAGE, DE 1994-96
Jamal Duff, DE 1997

93

Johnny Meads, LB 1992
Keith Willis, DT 1993
Jeff Faulkner, DT 1993
MARC BOUTTE, DT 1994-97

94

Anthony Sagnella, DT 1987
BOBBY WILSON, DT 1991-94
Sean Gilbert, DT 1996

95

Dan Benish, DT 1987
WILLIAM GAINES, DT 1995-97

96

Alec Gibson, DE 1987
Lamont Hollinquest, LB 1993-94
RICH OWENS, DE 1995-97

97

JUMPY GEATHERS, DT 1990-92
Sterling Palmer, DE 1993-96
Romeo Bandison, DT 1995-96
Kelvin Kinney, DE 1997

98

Steve Martin, DE 1987
Tony Barker, LB 1992
TONY WOODS, DE 1994-96
Twan Russell, LB 1997

99

EDDIE SAENZ, RB 1946-51
Wilbur Young, DE 1981
Ted Karras, DT 1987
Tracy Rocker, DT 1989-90
Jason Buck, DT 1991-93
Rod Stephens, LB 1995-96
Ryan Kuehl, DT 1996-97

RB LARRY BROWN (1969-76)   *Photo courtesy of the Washington Redskins*

ABOUT THE AUTHOR

David Elfin has covered the Redskins for six seasons for The Washington Times and is the co-author of "Hail To RFK: 36 Seasons of Redskins Memories" and "America's Rivalry: The 20 Greatest Redskins-Cowboys Games." Elfin, a native Washingtonian, is a graduate of the University of Pennsylvania and Syracuse University's Newhouse School. He has won numerous awards during his 16-year sportswriting career and serves on the board of directors of the Professional Football Writers of America. Elfin lives in Bethesda, Md. with his wife, Loretta Garcia, and their daughters, Julie and Amy.

AMERICA'S RIVALRY

The 20 Greatest Redskins-Cowboys Games

Remember the 1972 and 1982 NFC Championship victories over the Cowboys? How about Diron Talbert taunting Roger Staubach or Darrell Green defending Michael Irvin? Discover the real reasons behind the greatest rivalry in sports plus the All-Rivalry Team and photos from 20 games!

Just $12.95!

And don't forget Hail to RFK!
36 seasons of Redskins memories
in book ($11.95) or abridged audio tape ($19.95)

There's a 20% discount on multiple orders (Plus $5 shipping on first offer, $2 on additional offers)